Church of the English Martyrs, *c.* 1920. The Roman Catholic Church dedicated to the English Martyrs stands at the southern junction of Mitcham Lane and Tooting Bec Gardens. It was designed by A.E. Purdie and was built in 1892/3. The building to the right of the tower does not form part of the church and is an electricity substation. It was designed to be unobtrusive and blend in with its ecclesiastical surroundings. Note the Dyce fountain in its original location at the junction of Streatham High Road and Mitcham Lane (see p. 41).

THE TWENTIETH CENTURY
STREATHAM

PATRICK LOOBEY & JOHN W. BROWN

SUTTON PUBLISHING

First published in the United Kingdom in 2000 by
Sutton Publishing Limited · Phoenix Mill
Thrupp · Stroud · Gloucestershire · GL5 2BU

British Library Cataloguing in Publication Data
A catalogue record for this book is available from the British Library.

ISBN 0-7509-2619-8

Front endpaper: Streatham High Road looking north from the junction with Mitcham Lane,
c. 1900.
Title page photograph: Streatham Library, *c.* 1910.
Back endpaper: Streatham High Road looking north from the junction with Mitcham Lane,
1999.

*This book is dedicated to
Leslie William Brown.*

Typeset in 11/14 pt Photina.
Typesetting and origination by
Sutton Publishing Limited.
Printed and bound in England by
J.H. Haynes & Co. Ltd, Sparkford.

Contents

Streatham Hill Station, *c.* 1913.

St Leonard's Church, *c.* 1905.

Patrick Loobey, born in 1947, has lived in Balham, Putney, Southfields and Streatham – all within the Borough of Wandsworth. He joined the Wandsworth Historical Society (founded in 1953) in 1969 and has served on its archaeological, publishing and management committees, being chairman of the society from 1991 to 1994, and 1998 to 2001. Having collected Edwardian postcards of Wandsworth Borough and the surrounding district for more than twenty years, he has a wide-ranging collection of over 30,000 encompassing many local roads and subjects.

This book complements recent titles by Patrick covering the Borough of Wandsworth and surrounding areas, i.e. *Streatham* (1993 and 1996), *Battersea and Clapham* (1994 and 2000), *Balham and Tooting* (1994), *Wandsworth* (1993, 1994 and 1998), *Wandsworth and Battersea at War* (1996) and *Putney* (1988 and 1996). He has produced eighteen titles in all to date.

Reproductions of many of the views in this and other titles are available from Patrick Loobey, 231 Mitcham Lane, Streatham, London, SW16 6PY (Tel: 020 8769 0072).

John W. Brown was born in 1951 and has lived in Streatham all his life. His family has a long association with the area dating from the 1880s when his great-grandfather, John Brown, moved to the locality when it was a semi-rural country town on the outskirts of London.

His interest in local history was aroused when researching his family tree in response to pleas for help from relatives in America who were keen to learn about their British roots. His fascination with the subject was encouraged by his father who, when recalling his childhood adventures in Streatham at the time of the First World War, spoke of a rural locality which bore little resemblance to the busy London suburb that is Streatham today.

John has written numerous books on the history of Streatham and the surrounding area including *Streatham in Old Photographs, vols 1 and 2* (1993 and 1996), *Sherlock Holmes in Streatham* (1993), *Balham and Tooting in Old Photographs* (1994), *Streatham in Old Picture Postcards* (1998) and *Images of Streatham* (1999).

He publishes local history books and reprints of classic histories of the region written in the eighteenth and nineteenth centuries. He is a member of the Committee of the Local History Group of the Streatham Society, and belongs to numerous other local and family history organisations including the London Topographical Society and the Southwark and Lambeth Archaeological Society.

John lectures on local and family history as well as contributing articles on the subject to various journals and publications.

Leigham Court Estate Office at Streatham Hill, 1911. In 1891 the Artisans' Labourers and General Dwelling Company purchased a large mansion called Leigham Court which stood in extensive grounds at the southern end of Streatham Hill. They subsequently demolished the house and over the next thirty-seven years the grounds were developed as the Leigham Court Estate. The company set up an office at 107 Streatham Hill to market the houses that were free to let at modest rents. In 1911 maisonettes were available to rent for between £32 and £35 per annum.

Foreword

As both Mayor of Lambeth and a long-standing resident of Streatham I am delighted that the history of the area over the past 100 years is commemorated in *Streatham: The Twentieth Century*.

Through this fascinating collection of old photographs it is possible to glimpse something of the life and times of past residents and the diversity of Streatham's heritage.

Streatham is fortunate that so many of its fine buildings have survived the passing of the years and the ravages of war to provide such a rich townscape for us to appreciate today.

It is pleasing to know that in the final year of the twentieth century this has been recognised by the creation of a conservation area along Streatham Hill and Streatham High Road and that some of the best buildings in the area are now protected for the enjoyment of future generations.

Streatham is also fortunate in the diversity of its population which, together with its wide range of local groups and organisations, help make Streatham such a wonderful place in which to live, work or to visit.

The dawning of a new century provides a fitting time to reflect on the events of the past and assess the prospects for the future.

Over the past 100 years Streatham has developed from a small, semi-rural town into the bustling, vibrant south London suburb we see today.

With the appointment of a Streatham Town Centre Manager in 1996 and the recent approval of Heritage Economic Regeneration Scheme funding, Streatham can justifiably look forward to the future with increasing optimism and confidence.

Councillor Daphne Hayes Mojon
Mayor of Lambeth, 1998–9

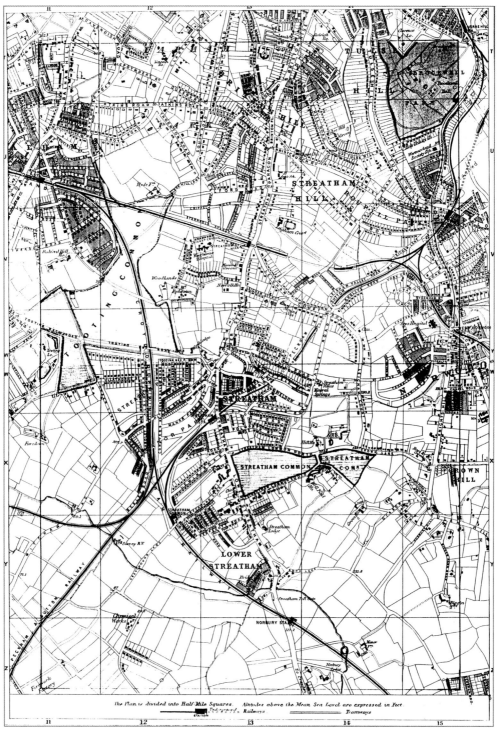

Map of Streatham, *c*. 1900. The ancient parish of Streatham stretched from Brixton Hill in the north to the southern banks of the River Graveney in the south, and from Balham and Tooting Bec in the west to Crown Lane in the east, with a small detached portion of the parish at Knights Hill. At the turn of the twentieth century this huge area had been subdivided into numerous parishes and distinct places within the old parish boundary, such as Balham and Tooting Bec, were no longer regarded as parts of Streatham.

Introduction

Avisitor to Streatham at the turn of the twentieth century would have discovered a delightful semi-rural town surrounded by fields and open pasture, and horse-drawn buses travelling to the area still had Streatham Village written on their destination boards.

In Valley Road cows from Curtis Brothers Dairy grazed the fields surrounding the old farmhouse in which glasses of Streatham's famous mineral water could still be obtained.

In the village the visitor would have seen a mixture of old and new buildings. Here and there a number of eighteenth-century cottages survived and along the High Road there were several large terraces of recently erected Victorian buildings, mainly stretching south from the junction with Mitcham Lane to Streatham Station. However, much of the High Road north of St Leonard's Church was still predominantly residential, with large detached houses standing in their own grounds.

Visitors would have been able to stroll in the centre of the High Road without fear of being run over by the traffic, and could have relaxed on Streatham Common with only the sound of the birds to disturb their peace. This was Streatham in 1900, an area still maintaining much of its rural charm.

The years leading up to the First World War were Streatham's halcyon days. A time when local residents could bask in the warm glow of their Edwardian affluence, enjoying a comfortable and prosperous lifestyle in a highly desirable residential area. However, events on the continent were soon to end this tranquil existence.

For Streatham the First World War was not just a distant conflict fought in the trenches of the Western Front, for on the night of 23/24 September 1916 a lone Zeppelin bombed the area leaving a trail of death and destruction in its wake. Other than the casualty lists in the local newspapers which recorded the 720 inhabitants of the parish who gave their lives in the First World War, the Zeppelin raid was to bring home to residents the harsh and brutal reality of twentieth-century warfare.

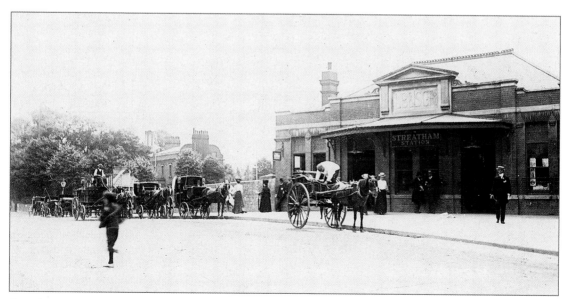

Streatham Station, *c.* 1908.

The years following the First World War were ones of continued development for Streatham and over the next twenty years the area was to be transformed from a semi-rural town into a bustling southern suburb of London.

A major development on the western side of Streatham Hill transformed the area into a leading entertainment centre for south London. The building of the Locarno Dance Hall, the Gaumont Picture Palace and the Streatham Hill Theatre consolidated Streatham's reputation as a fashionable and select place in which to live. This reputation was further enhanced with the building of large blocks of luxury flats along Streatham Hill and Streatham High Road. New roads of terraced housing accommodated a large army of London commuters and local shops thrived, attracting custom from far and wide.

As the Second World War approached, virtually the whole area had been developed. Streatham was now a built-up, densely populated suburb and the townscape as we now know it had been set in place.

At the outbreak of the war few fully realised the devastating effect the coming conflict was to have on the local community. During the Blitz, and the V1 attacks in the summer of 1944, an estimated 88 per cent of the buildings in Streatham were to suffer damage or destruction by enemy action. Many householders were fortunate in that their property suffered only minor harm with windows blown out or roof tiles lifted, but others saw their houses completely demolished or wrecked beyond repair.

As you wander around Streatham today you can still see an occasional 1950s house amid a row of Victorian or Edwardian terraced properties, the tell-tale sign of war damage. However, many of the 1930s houses that were destroyed were rebuilt to the same design and these wartime scars are now impossible to detect.

The immediate postwar years were ones of austerity and rebuilding for Streatham, but these soon gave way to a period of increasing prosperity for the neighbourhood. As the 1950s slipped into the 1960s, subtle changes began to emerge in Streatham that were to influence its future development. As elderly residents died or moved away, their large houses were converted into flats or bedsits to be occupied by younger residents; local organisations that once flourished found it hard to attract new members; and the local centres of entertainment found it difficult to compete with television. In 1965 a large portion of Streatham was transferred from the Borough of Wandsworth to Lambeth. By the 1980s the changing age, ethnic mix and social outlook of the local population resulted in different demands being placed on local traders and those who were slow to adapt found business increasingly difficult.

In 1990 the closure of Pratts Department Store, Streatham's largest shop, highlighted the impact these underlying social, cultural and commercial changes were having and signalled the passing of the 'old' Streatham, much lamented by long-standing residents of the area.

In the closing years of the twentieth century a 'new' Streatham began to emerge. Ballroom dancing and theatrical performances may no longer flourish at Streatham Hill, but Caesars nightclub, the Megabowl and Mayfair Bingo thrive by providing a new range of entertainments for a younger and more diverse clientele. Today, the High Road boasts a wide range of restaurants featuring cuisines from around the world, and more new pubs and wine bars have been opened in Streatham in the past 5 years than in the preceding 500.

At the dawn of a new century a fresh chapter begins in Streatham's history. For those wishing to learn more about the town's fascinating past a warm welcome awaits them at the meetings of the Local History Group of the Streatham Society. These are held at 8 p.m. on the first Monday of each month at Woodlawns, 16 Leigham Court Road, Streatham SW16. Illustrated talks on all aspects of Streatham's history are given, as well as workshop sessions, discussions and ephemera and collectable evenings at which members are encouraged to bring along items of interest.

I hope you will enjoy this photographic exploration of Streatham in the twentieth century and I would be delighted to hear from readers of their recollections of the area in days gone by.

John W. Brown
316 Green Lane
Streatham
London
SW16 3AS

Edwardian Streatham

Streatham High Road looking north from Mitcham Lane,
c. 1907. The dawn of the twentieth century saw
Streatham transformed from a small rural town into a
bustling London suburb. Within the space of a generation
the area had changed almost beyond recognition. The
open fields and pasture that once formed the Streatham
landscape was rapidly covered with houses and the High
Road became a thriving commercial centre. Streatham
was a prosperous and fashionable place in which to live
and local residents faced the challenges of the twentieth
century with great confidence and optimism.

Streatham High Road by Streatham Green. By the opening years of the twentieth century the High Road had changed completely. The small cottage properties that used to occupy this stretch of the road had been demolished and large, impressive buildings had been erected in their place. Spacious shops were at street level while above them were several floors of large flats providing comfortable accommodation. The High Road reflected the growing prosperity of the area and the windows of the new shops here were crowded with the latest consumer goods to entice trade.

Shops at Streatham Hill north of Leigham Court Road. The development of the Leigham Court Estate by the Artisans' Labourers and General Dwelling Company from 1891 onwards resulted in a large influx of new residents into the area. To cater for the commercial needs of the new population, the company incorporated shops in their properties fronting on to Streatham Hill between Leigham Court Road and Downton Avenue. Being located close to Streatham Hill Station this area quickly established itself as a popular shopping centre.

Sunnyhill Road School, *c.* 1901. This school was the first major public building to be erected in Streatham in the opening year of the twentieth century. A large gathering of local dignitaries assembled in the school hall in November 1900 when the new building was officially opened by the Revd W. Copeland Bowie, Chairman of the Accommodation Committee of the London School Board. This was the 444th school to be built by the Board at a total cost of about £26,000 providing places for 808 children.

Streatham Congregational Church, *c.* 1901. This was Streatham's new church for the new century. It was built on the site of a large house at 388 Streatham High Road called Heathfield that the Congregationalists had purchased in 1895. The house was subsequently demolished and on 16 May 1900 Mr Charles Derry, of the famous Derry & Toms department store, laid the foundation stone for the new church. This could accommodate 700 worshippers and was dedicated at a special service held on Tuesday 11 June 1901.

Streatham Fire Station, Mitcham Lane, *c.* 1904. The station was opened opposite Streatham Green in December 1903 by Mr Edward Smith, Chairman of the London County Council Fire Brigade Committee. It was built by Potter Brothers at a cost of £10,000 and housed a pump and a long escape ladder seen here. The firemen were accommodated in one- and two-bedroom flats situated on the three floors above the appliance room, with the Station Officer occupying a three-bedroom apartment on the first floor. Additional accommodation was provided at the rear of the station where four small cottages were erected. The building is now the South London Islamic Centre.

The King William IV, 1903. Travellers have been quenching their thirst in an inn at the junction of Streatham High Road and Hermitage Lane since at least the 1600s. The old pub that occupied this site was in a sorry state of repair by the end of the nineteenth century and in 1900 many complaints were received about the dreadful smell coming from its drains which were described as an 'intolerable nuisance' and 'a danger to health'. In 1903 Henry Mayes built a new pub which boasted a 'spacious and handsome' saloon bar, a billiard room with two tables and a smoking room. The rear garden was laid out as a bowling green and is now a beer garden and car park.

Norfolk House was one of the grand mansions of Streatham and occupied over 15 acres of gardens and parkland between Streatham High Road and Mount Ephraim Lane. A small lodge on the High Road guarded the entrance to the grounds and a long, sweeping carriage drive led to the house. At the rear of the property was a large lake (below) with a boathouse. In the centre of the lake was a small island which was a popular place for family picnics in the summer months. For many years Norfolk House was the home of Christopher Gabriel, a timber merchant, who died on 2 March 1873. Christopher's brother, Sir Thomas Gabriel, was Lord Mayor of London in 1866. The Gabriel family were wealthy and influential merchants and owned Gabriel's Wharf on the south bank of the Thames. After Christopher's widow, Ruth, died in 1898, the estate was sold. The house was subsequently demolished and in 1903 Norfolk House Road was laid out through the grounds.

Canon John Nicholl was Rector of Streatham from 1843 to 1904 and was the longest-serving vicar at St Leonard's Church, ministering to the parish for over sixty years. He was educated at Eton College and was appointed to the living at St Leonard's by the Duke of Bedford. During his ministry Canon Nicholl was responsible for the building of eighteen new churches in Streatham to cater for the spiritual needs of the increasing population of his parish. He died on 10 September 1905 aged ninety-six and is buried in the churchyard.

Streatham Rectory, c. 1905. The Rectory stood in Tooting Bec Gardens and was the home of the vicar of St Leonard's Church. Parts of the building dated back to at least 1535 when Thomas Martyn was the vicar. In the summer months the leading citizens of Streatham used to attend the fashionable garden parties that were held in the large grounds that surrounded the Rectory. The old Rectory, seen above, was demolished in 1907 and a new Rectory was built on the site with a church hall erected on part of the adjoining garden as a memorial to Canon John Nicholl.

Braxted Park, *c.* 1907. This road of fine Edwardian houses is typical of the large and impressive residences that were erected in Streatham in the opening years of the twentieth century. At that time Streatham was considered a highly desirable area in which to live. Roads such as Braxted Park attracted large numbers of wealthy residents into the area, who liked the spacious accommodation these houses provided as well as their location close to Streatham Common and Streatham Station.

Mrs Lillian Mummery and family stand in the doorway of her second-hand furniture and clothing shop at 261 Mitcham Lane in 1907. The photograph was sent to 'Grammar' by Phyllis, advising that 'Mama' was going to visit on Sunday with a 'nice big blouse and skirt' for her. Note the old treadle sewing machine on the pavement, probably used by Mrs Mummery to repair the clothes hanging in her shop window. The business did not prosper and was subsequently taken over by Frank Griffin who dispensed with the second-hand clothing and concentrated on selling furniture.

Note the ratio of boys to girls in this class photograph taken at Christ Church School, Streatham Hill, *c.* 1907. The school was built alongside Christ Church in 1844 and originally accommodated about 100 pupils. The day started with a scripture lesson, hymns and prayers. The youngest children had no exercise books and wrote with chalk on slates. Each child had to carry a damp rag or sponge with which to clean their slate and these were normally kept in small mustard tins with air-tight lids. Up until 1903 infants paid 2*d* (1p) a week towards the upkeep of the school with senior children paying 4*d* (2p).

On 27 May 1907 the Streatham Constitutional Club hosted an international bowls match against teams from Australia and New Zealand. The games were played on the green at the rear of the clubhouse that used to stand on the site now occupied by the Streatham Ice Arena. Although the Streatham side lost both their matches against the New Zealanders, and was also beaten on points by the Australians, the day was considered a great success. The festivities concluded that evening with a grand banquet for the players and their friends in the club dining room. The Constitutional Club is now based in Leigham Court Road.

Streatham cricketers, 1907. A group of Streatham cricketers pause from play to have their photograph taken outside a thatched hut, the location of which remains a mystery. The team consisted of local coachmen and gardeners who worked at some of the large houses in the area. Cricket has been a popular sport in Streatham since at least 1736 when mention is made of a match played on the 'White Lion Fields', which were probably near the White Lion public house, now known as the Hobgoblin. Streatham Cricket Club is one of the oldest in the country and was founded at the Horse and Groom (the present-day Big Hand Mo's pub) on 5 May 1806.

Christmas decorations in Streatham High Road, 1908. In Edwardian times Streatham was famous for its Christmas decorations. These were erected and paid for by local tradesmen who vied among themselves to mount the best yuletide window displays. In 1910 E.K. King's confectionery shop at 83 Streatham High Road won considerable praise for its windows, which contained 'a wonderful collection of the latest novelties suitable for the festive season, including an immense variety of bon-bons, Xmas crackers, and quaint and curious freak boxes containing choice confectionery'.

St Leonard's School, 1909. St Leonard's School in Mitcham Lane was rebuilt in 1909. The new school provided large, modern classrooms on two floors and replaced an older building that was erected in 1868 and can be seen on the left in the view below. The right-hand part of the old school was built in 1831 by the Kymer family who ran a charity school for girls at the premises. In 1838 Miss Kymer presented this school to the parish, together with a plot of land at the junction of Mitcham Lane and Ambleside Avenue on which a boys' school was built. In 1856 Miss Kymer made a further donation of a cottage and some land between the two schools which was used as an infant school. The infant school occupied this site until 1968 when it transferred to its present building further down Mitcham Lane, with the junior school completing the move in 1985. Ken Livingstone, former leader of the Greater London Council and the first elected Mayor of London, was a pupil at St Leonard's School in the 1950s at which time he was living at 21b Shrubbery Road.

Laying tramlines at Streatham Common in 1909.
Throughout the early months of 1909 Streatham High Road was the scene of much activity as the tram service was extended from Streatham Library to Hermitage Bridge. The work involved caused considerable inconvenience with the road being dug up for many months while workmen laid the new tram lines. The extended tram service began operations in July and carried passengers to the Croydon tram terminus that was situated on the southern side of the River Graveney where London Road, Norbury, becomes Streatham High Road.

Empire Cinema, 1910. One of the most popular entertainments for Streatham residents in the opening decade of the twentieth century was the cinema. Silent films, often screened to the accompaniment of dramatic piano music, drew huge crowds. To cater for this demand a number of cinemas were built in Streatham. One of the largest of these was the Empire, which can be seen on the extreme right of this view, next to the Bedford Park public house. This cinema could accommodate 1,200 patrons and was opened in December 1910. The cinema hall survives today as Potters Snooker Club.

Henry Hird, standing in the centre wearing a straw boater, on the bowling green situated behind the Crown and Sceptre public house at Streatham Hill, *c.* 1911. The Crown Bowling Club were proud of their green and the thatched hut, seen on the right, which they used as a club house. The club staged various tournaments here and the pub's close proximity to the green made it a popular venue for other bowling clubs to visit. Note the classical statues standing among the hedges between the public house and club hut. Henry Hird owned a builder's and ironmonger's business in Balham and died in January 1915.

A magnificent display of early motor vehicles stand on a small plot of land between Nos 43 and 45 Mitcham Lane, *c.* 1912. The workshops for the Station Motor Garage were situated here with the company's main office being at 376 Streatham High Road, near Streatham Railway Station. Prior to the opening of Streatham Fire Station in 1903 (see p. 4) a temporary fire station was established here. This site was used as a garage and motor workshops for most of the twentieth century and is currently occupied by a Kwik-Fit centre.

Streatham Rovers Cycling Club, 1912. The club was founded in about 1905 and normally met on Sundays at a local pub. After refreshment the cyclists would head out to such places as Lingfield and Ashtead in Surrey, where they would sample the beverages to be had at a local hostelry before beginning their return journey to Streatham. In addition to such trips, various speed trials and races were held for which a cup was awarded. This can be seen in the photograph and was presented to the club by Harry Lee, the licensee of the King William IV public house (see p. 4).

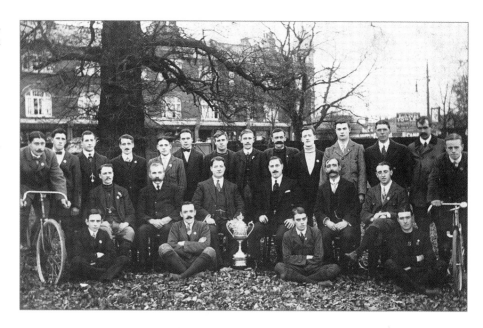

Streatham Police Station at the junction of the High Road and Shrubbery Road, 1912. A police station has occupied this site on Streatham High Road since 1865. After much agitation by locals over the cramped conditions endured by the local force the old station was demolished in 1912 and replaced with the red-brick building seen here. The upper floors of the new station provided quarters for married staff, with single policemen being accommodated in a section house which was built in Shrubbery Road in 1914. Note the Thrale Almshouses on the right (see p. 46).

Local dignitaries gather at Streatham Library on Saturday 5 October 1912 for the unveiling of the King Edward VII Memorial Clock by the Mayor of Wandsworth, Alderman Archibald Dawnay. The clock was made by Gillett and Johnston of Croydon and was designed by Mr A. St Hill Brock, FRIBA, of 6 Duke Street, Adelphi, London. The mechanism is enclosed in a handsome case constructed of Moulmein teak on the end panel of which is carved the Imperial Crown, beneath which is the royal cipher surrounded by a wreath of oak leaves.

It was an unlucky day for this tram on 13 November 1913, when it came to grief at the junction of Mitcham Lane and Southcroft Road. It was not carrying passengers at the time and only the driver, Albert Attridge, and conductor, Sidney Mellars, were on board. As it travelled down Mitcham Lane the tram gradually built up speed and on entering the bend into Southcroft Road the brakes failed and it toppled over. Miraculously Albert was able to jump clear of the vehicle before it crashed, but unfortunately Sidney was not so lucky and was seriously injured.

Members of the Streatham Amateur Operatic Society in costume. In the years leading up to the First World War amateur dramatics and musical recitals were popular pastimes for many Streatham residents. Numerous local clubs and societies catered for such activities and one of the best known of these was the Streatham Amateur Operatic Society. This group was formed in the early 1890s and their productions of the operas of Gilbert and Sullivan were extremely popular and always attracted large and appreciative audiences.

The Rookery Gardens, 1913. The Rookery was a large house erected in 1786 near the site of Streatham Mineral Wells, which were discovered here in 1659. The house was acquired by the London County Council in 1912 which demolished the building and refurbished the surrounding grounds that were opened as public gardens in 1913. A 'wishing well' (above) survives in the centre of the gardens and is one of three original wells that at one time supplied the medicinal waters for which Streatham was famous in the seventeenth and eighteenth centuries. Following the opening of the Rookery it became fashionable to stroll in the gardens on a Sunday afternoon and in the summer months the grounds would be full of local residents. Ladies would parade here in their fine clothes and bonnets and gentlemen would wear smart suits and either straw boaters or bowler hats. Children would don their 'Sunday best', which for many young boys took the form of a sailor suit as seen in the picture below.

The First World War

NATIONAL VOLUNTEER RESERVE.

STREATHAM UNIT.

SOUTH LONDON BATTALION

(Affiliated to Central Association Volunteer Training Corps).

If you are Eligible for His

Majesty's Regular Forces,

WE DON'T WANT YOU.

If you are not,

WE DO!

COME AND ENROL

At Headquarters,

5th EAST SURREY DRILL HALL

Estreham Road

(Opposite Streatham Common Station)

Streatham National Volunteer Reserve poster, 1915. The First World War brought to an end the confidence and prosperity of the Edwardian era. Local residents were quick to support the war effort and many men who were not eligible to enlist in the armed services joined the local contingent of the National Volunteers. The initial optimism that the war would be 'over by Christmas' quickly faded and the early jingoism of 1914 was replaced by a more sombre mood as the casualties rose on the Western Front.

IMPORTANT NOTICE !!

To the Inhabitants of Streatham

£5 REWARD.

The above REWARD will be paid to anyone giving us information which will enable us to discover the person responsible for sending out Post Cards to many of the inhabitants of Streatham which contained the following:

" Bread made by Germans can be obtained at
Paul & Callard's, 128 High Road, Streatham."

We have not employed a German Bread Baker for Sixteen Years. The only Foreign Confectioner we have had during this period is one who has been in England since his youth (25 years), and whose - - relations are or were before the siege - at Liege.

We trust you will do all in your power to assist us to unearth this anonymous coward.

PAUL & CALLARD,

314 High Road, Streatham.

Telephone · Streatham 64.

With the outbreak of war there was a marked increase in anti-German feeling in Streatham. This manifested itself in an unusual incident in September 1914 when a large number of postcards were sent to local residents advising that 'Bread made by Germans can be obtained at Paul & Callard's, 128 High Road, Streatham'. Such was the impact on the baker's trade that he was forced to place this advertisement in the *Streatham News* refuting all such claims. Readers were advised that the firm had not employed a 'German Bread Baker' for sixteen years and a reward of £5 was offered to anyone helping to identify the 'anonymous coward' who was spreading such rumours.

Christopher Brown, whose family lived in Colmer Road, proudly wears a child's soldier's uniform and Queen Alexandra's Medal. Some 1,300 children, aged eight to thirteen, and whose fathers were serving in the Army or Navy, were presented with the medal at a banquet for 'Little Londoners' hosted by the Lord Mayor of London at the Guildhall on 28 December 1914. The children feasted on a banquet of roast beef, plum pudding, fruit and milk and were presented with gifts of sweets, crackers and toys. The medal bears the inscription 'Fear God and Honour the King'. At the time of the presentation Christopher's father, William Charles Brown, was serving with the British Expeditionary Force in France.

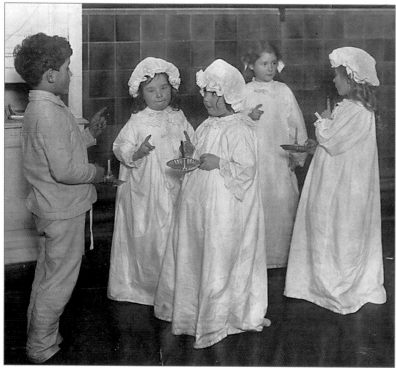

In 1915 the Mayor of Wandsworth, Sir Archibald Dawnay, launched an appeal to raise money for a motor ambulance for use by the 13th Wandsworth Battalion. Various fund-raising events were held throughout the borough and in Streatham a 'grand entertainment' was given by the pupils at the Streatham Secondary Training College and Furzedown schools in Welham Road. A highlight of the production was the performance given by the infants, seen here dressed in their night-clothes, for their rendition of 'The Dance of Good Night'.

Streatham Rifle Club
SPECIAL NOTICE.
THERE will be a Drill in the Pendennis Road Cricket Ground (wet or fine), at 3.30 next Saturday afternoon, the 10th Oct., and at 11 on the Sunday morning following. Competent Instructors will be in attendance. Your presence is urgently needed for purposes of preliminary organisation.

HEADQUARTERS:
9 MITCHAM LANE   STREATHAM

Streatham Rifle Club poster, 1914. The Streatham Rifle Club was formed on 8 September 1914 by local men who wanted to help the war effort. Akin to the 'Home Guard' in the Second World War, the club mainly comprised men who were too old for active military service. An announcement in the local press about the formation of the club met with an overwhelming response and by the end of October over 1,500 men had enlisted. The club had its original headquarters at 9 Mitcham Lane, and drilled on Streatham and Tooting Bec Commons, as well as the Streatham Cricket Club ground in Pendennis Road.

As a result of the success of the Streatham Rifle Club it was decided to affiliate the group with the Central Association of Volunteer Corps, and the Streatham Volunteer Training Corps (SVTC) came into existence. A vice-president of the Streatham Rifle Club was Sir Herbert Parsons, of Winton Lodge, Crown Lane, seen here sitting in his car when visiting the SVTC at their Whitsun camp in 1915. Sir Herbert took his car and chauffeur to France in 1914–15 where he assisted the Red Cross in conveying the wounded to hospital. From 1911 to 1923 he was Hon. Colonel of the 3rd (City of London) Battalion, and raised two battalions of the London regiment during the war.

Streatham Volunteer Training Corps' 1915 Whitsun camp. The corps was initially based at the Drill Hall in Estreham Road which was also the headquarters of the 2nd Volunteer Battalion of the 5th East Surrey Regiment. The corps was commanded by Major H.M. Warne, of Ambleside Avenue, and the unit comprised four companies each having its own company commander. A drum and bugle band accompanied the volunteers on church parades and marches, the instruments being donated by the corps' Hon. Commandant, Mr G.H.L. Parsons, of Aldrington Road, Streatham Park. At the Whitsun training camp the men slept in bell tents, as seen on the left of the picture below. While at camp the men participated in various manoeuvres and exercises to improve their military proficiency and prepare them for active duty in the event of Britain being invaded by the enemy.

Curtis dairymaids, *c.* 1916. As the war progressed the only way the Army's increasing demands for manpower could be met was through the introduction of conscription. With so many able-bodied men volunteering or being called to the colours, women had to perform traditionally male tasks to keep the wheels of industry and commerce turning. As well as becoming 'clippies' on the buses and assuming a more prominent role in serving customers in shops, they increasingly provided the bulk of the labour force for factories producing war supplies. In Streatham, the milkman soon disappeared from local streets to be replaced by 'milkmaids' who took over their rounds. These photographs show two of the women employed at that time by Curtis Brothers Dairy in Valley Road. The job of a dairy maid was a hard one involving rising at dawn to milk the cows before completing the early morning milk round, after which there were more cows to milk and another round to complete.

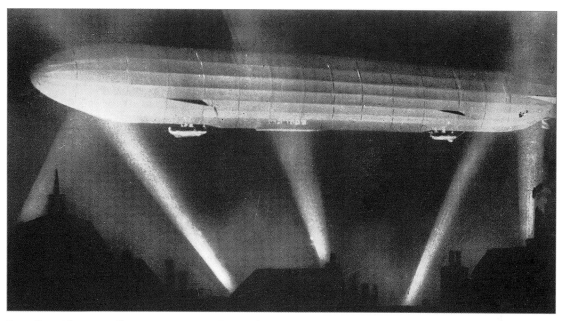

Zeppelin raids were still a rare occurrence for Londoners when Streatham was 'hit by the Hun' on the night of 23/24 September 1916. Only five previous raids had been successfully mounted against the capital in the preceding sixteen months of the war. As Zeppelin *L31* journeyed over Streatham it left a trail of death and destruction in its wake. Residents first became aware of the raid when they heard the explosion of three bombs that landed in the goods yard of Streatham Common Station. A railway truck and two wagons were blown to pieces and a shunting cabin and loading dock, seen below, were damaged. Opposite the station a high-explosive bomb wrecked numbers 10–14 Estreham Road where Mrs Mary Chadwick, a pensioner, was killed. During the 15 minutes of the raid the Zeppelin dropped 32 bombs, killing a total of 7 people and seriously injuring a further 27.

The worst incident of the 1916 Zeppelin raid occurred outside Streatham Hill Station. A bomb exploded in the garden of the Streatham Hill Modern School at 70 Streatham Hill, at the corner of Sternhold Avenue. A tramcar standing in the halted traffic outside the station caught the full force of the explosion. The intensity of the blast was such that four men on board the tram were killed instantly, including the conductor, Charles Boys, and the driver, T. Gaymer. Another passenger, William Wood, was fatally injured and died soon after being admitted to hospital. A large crowd, seen left, gathered at the station later that morning to view the damage. The tram was based at the Telford Avenue depot and the photograph below shows the funeral procession of the conductor and driver as it passed along Streatham Hill on 29 September 1916.

Streatham allotments, *c.* 1917. To supplement limited food supplies local residents were encouraged to 'dig for victory'. Many inhabitants turned their gardens into vegetable plots and a number of local clubs and 'cultivation societies' were formed to help provide additional produce. Areas of wasteland were soon brought under cultivation and the photograph above shows the allotments situated alongside the railway line near Streatham Common Station. One of the largest and most enthusiastic of Streatham's allotment groups was the Furzedown Cultivation Society. They planted a large area of vacant land to the north of Welham Road on which a variety of vegetables and fruit was grown. The picture below shows members of the Society in 1919 armed with their spades and forks in the grounds of what is now Graveney School.

LOOK YOU!

EXCELLENT   SMOKED

BACK   1/1 D

OR   Per lb.

STREAKY

BACON   1/-   Per lb.

UNSMOKED

Sliced by Patent Machine.

NOW DON'T SIT DOWN AND GROUSE,
BUT COME ALONG AND BUY.

We Have Enough for Everybody.

WORLD'S STORES,

101 MITCHAM LANE, STREATHAM, S.W.

Furzedown Pig Club, 1919. With the introduction of rationing in 1917 the demand for locally grown produce to supplement food supplies increased. Various pig, poultry and rabbit clubs received a new lease of life to help provide fresh meat. Some members of the Furzedown Cultivation Society formed a pig club and through the generosity of a local landowner, Sir Charles Seeley, they built sties on his land to house their livestock. The buildings were made of wood and stood on solid concrete floors with 'a perfect system of drainage' to ensure a minimum of smells for the public and maximum comfort for the pigs. The sties were inaugurated by the Mayor of Wandsworth, Sir Archibald Dawnay, in 1918. Left, an advert from the 5 January 1917 edition of the *Streatham News* extols the bacon bargains to be had at World's Stores at 101 Mitcham Lane.

Workers preparing field dressings at the Streatham War Hospital Supply Depot, 1916. The depot was based in a large mansion called Hill House that stood on Streatham Common North, opposite the upper pond on the Common. Following the outbreak of war the house was used to accommodate Belgian refugees and in 1915 the owner of the property, Mr Newton Dunn, made it available for use as a War Hospital Supply Depot. At its peak up to 1,200 local volunteers worked here producing items for use in treating war casualties in Britain and in field hospitals overseas. Each volunteer contributed 1s (5p) a week to the depot's general fund for the purchase of materials. The depot was the second largest of its type in the country and by the end of the war it had produced 684,276 items valued then at £57,731. Surgical supplies made at Hill House went to hospitals as far afield as Alexandria, Milan, Petrograd, Cannes and Malta. On the right is a photograph of Lady Parsons (wife of Sir Herbert Parsons, see page 20) who was one of the chief organisers at the depot.

HM Queen Alexandra. On 10 May 1916 Queen Alexandra made an official visit to Streatham with Princess Victoria and Princess Arthur of Connaught. The royal party attended a children's pageant to celebrate the first anniversary of the opening of the War Hospital Supply Depot at Hill House. The Queen had previously made a private visit to the depot on 18 August 1915 when she met many of the volunteers working there. She made her third visit to Streatham on 25 May 1917 to attend a patriotic sale and concert at Streatham Hall to mark the second anniversary of the depot's opening.

Major Frederick Henry Johnson VC, of Streatham, was awarded his Victoria Cross for 'most conspicuous bravery and devotion to duty' in the attack on Hill 70 in France, on 25 September 1915. Although wounded in the leg he led several charges on the German redoubt and at a very critical time in the action, while under heavy fire, repeatedly rallied the men who were near him. 'By his splendid example and cool courage' he was instrumental in saving the situation and in securing that part of the line that he and his comrades had captured. Frederick Johnson was born on 15 August 1890 at 13 Bedford Row, now 157 Streatham High Road, where his father, Samuel Rogers Johnson, ran a confectionery shop (see p. 71). Major Johnson was killed in action in France on 26 November 1917.

The Chimes, *c.* 1922. As part of Streatham's War Memorial, The Chimes, a large house that stood on the corner of Streatham High Road and Streatham Common North, was purchased for use as a United Services Club for war veterans. The building was named after a clock on the house which used to chime every quarter of an hour and could be heard across the Common. The building was probably erected in the early 1860s and from the late 1870s to the mid-1880s was the home of Major Alfred Heales, a noted archaeologist and Fellow of the Society of Antiquaries. It later became the residence of Sir Horace Brooks Marshall, Lord Mayor of London in 1918–19. He allowed the house to be used as a home for Belgian refugees during the First World War, which was visited by HRH the Duchess de Vendome, sister of the King of the Belgians. On 5 July 1944 a V1 bomb fell nearby seriously damaging the building and it was subsequently demolished. A block of flats forming part of Albert Carr Gardens was erected on the site after the war.

Streatham War Memorial, 1922. The bronze statue of a lone soldier, his head bowed and his hands resting on an upturned rifle – a military sign of mourning – commemorates the 720 inhabitants of Streatham who lost their lives in the First World War. The memorial stands at the junction of Streatham High Road and Streatham Common North. It was unveiled by General Sir Charles Munro on 14 October 1922 before a crowd of about 5,000 local residents. The memorial was designed by Albert T. Toft and identical statues by the same sculptor are also to be found at Stone in Staffordshire, Leamington in Warwickshire and Thornton Cleveleys in Lancashire.

Between the Wars

Streatham Hill in the mid-1930s. The period between the wars witnessed the final phase of the suburbanisation of Streatham. At Streatham Hill a major development north of the railway station, on the western side of the road, was to see the area transformed into a leading entertainment centre with the building of the Locarno Dance Hall, the Gaumont Palace Cinema and the Streatham Hill Theatre. Such major recreational attractions did much to consolidate Streatham's reputation as a popular residential area.

Following the First World War a block of shops and flats was erected on the corner of Sternhold Avenue and Streatham Hill. The building occupies the site of Streatham Hill Modern School which was gutted by the Zeppelin bomb that fell here in 1916 (see p. 24). The plain style of the building is in stark contrast to the more ornate premises erected on the east side of Streatham Hill by the Artisans' Labourers and General Dwelling Company about thirty years earlier and is typical of the new buildings erected in Streatham at this time.

The staff of Welford's Dairies stand proudly outside their shop on the corner of Gracedale and Moyser Roads in 1920. A sign painted across the windows assures customers that 'absolutely pure milk from our own farms' is sold on the premises. A large stuffed bird can be seen in the window promoting the produce on display. Welford's Surrey Dairies Ltd operated a number of outlets in the area and some of their cows grazed at Furzedown Park Farm from the 1880s until 1905 when the farm buildings were demolished and Ramsdale Road was built on the site.

Green Lane looking towards Streatham High Road, 1922. The North Surrey Golf Club covered much of the land at the western end of Green Lane. In the early 1920s Wates Ltd began building here and two blocks of terraced houses were erected between Streatham High Road and Strathbrook Road in 1922. Mr Geoffrey Page, who purchased what is now 314 Green Lane, was taken to the junction with Strathbrook Road by Mr Wates who showed him the grounds of the golf course that he would be able to enjoy within yards of his new house. However, within a few years much of the land there had also been built on by Mr Wates who developed it as the Green Lane Estate.

Telford Avenue Tram Depot. The tram service reached Streatham Hill in the early 1890s and by 1909 it had been extended along Streatham Hill and Streatham High Road as far as Hermitage Bridge. To help maintain the tram cars the London County Council built a repair shed in 1923 on the site of a large Victorian residence called Aspen House that stood near the northern junction of Streatham Hill and Christchurch Road. When the trams were scrapped in 1951 the tram depot was pulled down and Brixton Hill Bus Garage was erected in its place. The repair shed subsequently became Stratstone Garage but the building is now empty and its future use is uncertain.

Streatham Vale, *c.* 1926. The Streatham Vale Estate was one of the largest of the interwar housing developments and was laid out on land on the western side of the Streatham Common Railway line. This was at one time considered unsuitable for house building and was mainly used for market gardening as it was subject to flooding in heavy rains and was very boggy in places. Streatham Vale was formerly known as Lonesome Lane and led to a desolate area on the Streatham/Mitcham borders known as Lonesome, which signified its remote and isolated location.

St Paul's Church, Furzedown, 1926. Situated in Welham Road, the church was consecrated by the Bishop of Southwark, Dr Cyril Garbett, on 21 September 1926. It was the first church to be built in the diocese after the First World War and cost £12,248. Over 1,000 people attended the dedication service and, as the church was only designed to accommodate 615 worshippers, it was 'crowded to the utmost capacity'. The building is in a simple thirteenth-century style, built mainly of brick and stone, with fine lancet windows which give the church a very dignified, spacious and lofty appearance.

Granton Road School, 1928. To provide education for the children of the families moving into Streatham Vale, a new primary school was built in Granton Road, seen in this early aerial view of the area. The school was erected in 1928 and was designed to accommodate 604 pupils: 280 juniors and 324 infants. In addition to providing daytime tuition for young children, the building was used by an Evening Institute and the hall was hired for dances and socials on Saturday evenings by the Streatham Vale Sports and Social Club.

Streatham Swimming Baths, Streatham High Road, 1927. The baths stand on the site of an old house used by Wandsworth Council as a Rate Office and Coroner's Court. The foundations for the baths were dug in 1924 as part of the council's unemployment relief scheme. However, construction was delayed as housing requirements took preference for the supply of building materials. Work was further held up by the 1926 General Strike and it was not until 28 September 1927 that the Mayor, Alderman S. Cresswell, was able to officially declare the baths open for public use.

The Locarno, Streatham Hill. On Tuesday 1 October 1929 about 1,500 people gathered at the Locarno Dance Hall for its opening night. Sadly, Ivy Tresmand, a well-known musical comedy actress who was to perform the opening ceremony, was indisposed and unable to attend. However, Dorothy Seacombe, another popular actress of the day, undertook this duty to rapturous applause from the assembled crowd. To lilting music supplied by Billy Mayerl's orchestra, couples took to the floor for a foxtrot and the Locarno burst into life as one of London's premier dance halls.

The Streatham Hill Theatre. The second of Streatham's major entertainment amenities to open in the interwar years was the Streatham Hill Theatre. This was one of London's largest suburban theatres accommodating 2,600 patrons, more than could be housed in such famous West End venues as the Opera House, Covent Garden or the Drury Lane Theatre. The first performance took place on 20 November 1929 when Jessie Matthews and Sonnie Hale starred in *Wake Up and Dream*. The theatre was badly damaged by a V1 bomb on 3 July 1944 and was closed (see p. 58). It reopened on Boxing Day 1950 but closed again in June 1962 when it was converted into a Bingo Hall (see p. 105).

Harvest Festival, 1930. Although by the 1930s Streatham had ceased to be considered a rural parish, the Harvest Festival was still a major occasion and was celebrated in both schools and churches. Here children at Christ Church School, Streatham Hill, hand over their harvest gifts to the headmaster, Mr F. Wood. Among the items being donated are a can of Argus peaches in golden syrup, jars of home-made jam, tins of sardines, packets of Tate & Lyle sugar, and numerous cartons of Quaker Oats and Breakfast Oats. Note the small child on the far right with the large marrow.

The Astoria Cinema on the northern junction of Streatham High Road and Pendennis Road. One of the highlights of 1930 was the opening of the Astoria Cinema on 30 June. Designed by E.A. Stone, the interior drew considerable praise for its modelling on an Egyptian theme. It was painted in 'pleasing tones' of red, green and gold, which were enhanced by carefully concealed and reflected lighting. The flank walls of the circle were enriched with highly coloured bas-reliefs of Egyptian scenes and the 2,500 people who attended the opening night marvelled at the magnificence of the building. It is now a five-screen Odeon cinema.

The Greyhound public house, 1930. Since the early eighteenth century at least four pubs called the Greyhound have occupied this site at the top of Greyhound Lane. The Greyhound was rebuilt in 1930 for Charles Walter Hoye who landscaped the gardens at the rear of the inn to provide 'Streatham's Finest Garden Rendezvous!' Patrons were advised that this 'select rendezvous, which has a spacious car park, will appeal to all in search of refreshment under the most pleasant and approved conditions. For rest and refreshment it is the traveller's Mecca.'

Pupils at New Park Road School were on their best behaviour when this photograph was taken in 1930/1. No doubt the presence of the teacher, Mr Richard Oxford, standing at the back of the class was enough to ensure good order. The school was built in 1897 and is now known as Richard Atkins School. A former pupil here was Harold John Milford who, while serving as a flight lieutenant in the Second World War, was shot down and captured by the Germans. He was one of the POWs to escape from Stalag Luft III in 1944 and was among the forty-seven who were shot dead on recapture. The break-out was depicted in the film *The Great Escape*.

Members of the 92nd London Company, The Boys' Brigade, 1931. There was a marked growth in membership of uniformed youth organisations after the First World War. The 92nd London Company was established at St Andrew's Church, Guildersfield Road, in September 1929. For many years it was led by its founder, Captain 'Archie' Milan (seated centre), under whose guidance it flourished. In the 1930s the company headquarters was transferred to the upper floor of St Andrew's School Hall in Colmer Road (see p. 103) from where it provided a wide range of activities for local boys for over fifty years.

Streatham Ice Rink, c. 1931. The Mayor of Wandsworth, Lieutenant Colonel Bellamy, supported by the MP for Streatham, Sir William Lane-Mitchell, opened the Streatham Ice Rink on 26 February 1931. The rink was designed by Robert Cromie and its 21,000 square feet of ice can accommodate 1,000 skaters. In 1935 the rink appeared in the film *Car of Dreams* starring John Mills, and in 1937 the American film star Robert Taylor learned to skate here for his part in the film *A Yank at Oxford*. The rink was later known as The Silver Blades and survives today as The Streatham Ice Arena.

The Gaumont Palace Cinema at Streatham Hill opened on 14 March 1932 with the screening of *Michael and Mary* starring Herbert Marshall and Edna Best. With seating for 2,431 patrons the cinema was one of the largest in the area. The building closed after suffering serious damage from enemy bombing in 1942 and did not reopen until July 1955. The cinema screened its last film, *Breath of Scandal* starring Sophia Loren and Maurice Chevalier, in March 1961 after which it was converted into the Streatham Bowl, the largest ten-pin bowling alley outside the USA (see p. 98).

Woodmansterne Road School was the second school to be built on the Streatham Vale Estate and occupies a large area of land at the rear of Woodmansterne and Stockport Roads. Built in 1930, the school is a single-storey building with a central hall. It was designed to accommodate 864 children: 232 infants, 320 juniors and 312 seniors. This photograph shows the school's successful netball team in 1932 with the headmaster, Mr Rowson, and the netball teacher, Miss Herriman, standing on the right.

Dyce Fountain (centre) was originally erected at the junction of Streatham High Road and Mitcham Lane in 1862. When the land at the rear was redeveloped in 1933 it was moved to its present position on Streatham Green. The fountain was designed by William Dyce who was churchwarden of St Leonard's from 1862 to 1864. Dyce was a noted artist of his day and a pioneer of the Pre-Raphaelite movement. In addition to painting he also designed the Victorian florin or *2s* piece, the equivalent of the modern-day 10p coin. Dyce died on St Valentine's day 1864 and is buried in St Leonard's graveyard.

Wavertree Court was erected in 1933/4 on the site of two large Georgian houses, Nos 37 and 39 Streatham Hill. From 1838 to 1855 Alderman Thomas Kelly, the publisher and bookseller, lived at No. 39, and Dennis Wheatley, the famous occult novelist, spent his early boyhood at no. 37, *c.* 1903–6. One of Wavertree Court's best-known former residents is the actor Roger Moore, who moved here with his first wife, Lucy Woodard, soon after they were wed in 1946. Their marriage was short-lived and ended in 1952 after Roger's affair with the singer Dorothy Squires, whom he married in 1953.

The Shrubbery was a large eighteenth-century house that stood on Streatham High Road. It was built in 1768 by the Revd James Tattersall, Rector of Streatham between 1754 and 1784. In 1894 the Church School Society established a girls' school here which was later known as Streatham College for Girls. The school was nicknamed the 'Snobbery' by local children due to the refined nature of its students. The photograph below shows a classroom which at one time was used as the headquarters of the Streatham Lodge; hence the fireplace bearing various Masonic symbols. The school had large gardens to the front and rear and its prime location in the heart of Streatham led to the property being demolished in 1935 when the site was redeveloped with shops and flats called Central Parade.

Pullman Court, 1936. This was one of the most luxurious blocks of flats to be built in Streatham between the wars and was constructed in 1935 in the grounds of the former Royal Asylum of St Anne's Society Home. Designed by Sir Frederick Gibberd, Pullman Court contains 218 units in 3 blocks, ranging from 3 to 7 storeys in height. The estate incorporates landscaped grounds and an outdoor swimming pool. Pullman Court is a Grade II* listed building and is widely considered to be one of the finest examples of 1930s architecture in south London.

Residents of Danbrook Road don their party hats to celebrate the coronation of King George VI and Queen Elizabeth in 1936. The road was festooned with flags to mark the occasion and red, white and blue streamers and bunting decorated the street. Children enjoyed a slap-up tea and party games. The day ended with the adults toasting the new King and Queen's health with ample supplies of ale and spirits. It is assumed that the photographer also liberally celebrated the event as his focus is a little fuzzy in this picture.

Bertram Cowen Motors, Hermitage Lane, 1938. The 1920s and 1930s were to see horse-drawn vehicles on the streets of Streatham largely replaced by motorised transport. To cater for the needs of the increasing number of car owners many new garages were established in the area. Among these was Bertram Cowen's garage in Hermitage Lane, south Streatham. As well as providing service, breakdown and repair work, he also sold a range of new and second-hand vehicles in a car showroom which continues to trade today as Hermitage Motors.

Residents and friends gather in the hall at the British Home and Hospital for Incurables for a 'High Tea' in the 1930s. The chaplain, standing centre left, and some of the nurses can be seen chatting to guests while they wait to be served. Note the lady musicians seated on the stage resting between performances. The hospital was founded in 1861 for the 'relief of incurable diseases, accident or deformity'. It was originally based in Clapham and moved to Streatham in 1894 when the Prince and Princess of Wales opened the new hospital in Crown Lane on 3 July.

The High, Streatham High Road, *c.* 1938. The High was designed by Toms & Partners and was originally to comprise 124 flats and 22 shops. However, as work progressed the size of the flats shrunk and their number was increased to 174. An advertisement in 1937 advises prospective tenants they could enjoy a swimming pool, a residents' club with facilities for dancing and refreshments, a billiards room, table tennis, 'Electric Passenger and Tradesmen's lifts', constant softened hot water, uniformed porters and garages, all for a rental of between £80 and £130 a year!

Bill Watts and the White Aces producing their syncopated rhythm at the Sussex public house in Streatham. An old beer shop called the 'Sussex' operated from the southern corner of Colmer and Streatham High Roads until 1937 when a full licence was granted to a new pub of that name built beside Hermitage Bridge. Dancing was a popular pastime in the 1920s and '30s and dances were held regularly on Saturday evenings at various local halls. Bill Watts lived in Ellison Road and is seated left playing the trumpet with Wallie and Archie on the extreme right playing their saxophones.

The Thrale Almshouses (seen above) were built on Streatham High Road in 1832 by the surviving daughters of Henry and Hester Thrale of Streatham Park, and Henry Hoare, the widower of their seventh child, Sophia Thrale. The almshouses provided subsidised lodgings for four poor widows or single women who had 'attained an honest old age' in Streatham. The building was demolished in 1930 when the land was sold for redevelopment. In their place eight new homes, designed by Cecil M. Quilter, were erected in Polworth Road (see below). In 1939, following the death of Lady Edith Robinson, the wife of the president of the Streatham Conservative Association, it was decided to erect additional accommodation in her memory and £1,000 was raised which covered the cost of building two new almshouses on the Polworth Road site.

The Second World War

A barrage balloon on Streatham Common, 1939. Following the outbreak of the Second World War, Streatham was full of activity as the Civil Defence authorities prepared for the conflict. The digging of air-raid shelters in public places continued; kerbstones and the bottom of lamp-posts and telegraph poles were painted white to make them more noticeable in the blackout. On Streatham Common a barrage balloon was installed and flown at a height of about 5,000 ft to deter low-level attacks by enemy aircraft. Few inhabitants fully appreciated the impact the war would have on life in Streatham or the level of casualties and destruction that the suburb would suffer in the ensuing five years.

Woodmansterne School evacuation to Wales, 1939. An early wartime precaution was the evacuation of school children to country areas that were unlikely to suffer from heavy bombing. Pupils from Woodmansterne School were decamped to the small Carmarthenshire village of Llanwdra, near Llandovery, in Wales. Some attended the local Welsh school, seen here, and ended the war speaking quite good Welsh. Other pupils went to an 'English School' run by Miss Joliffe and Miss Jennings. Note that each child is carrying their gas mask in the cardboard box provided by the authorities.

The men of Streatham step forward in 1939 to enrol in the Local Defence Volunteers, later to be known as the Home Guard. About 3,500 local men served in the 31st London (Streatham) Battalion of the Home Guard with 1,000 subsequently going on to join the armed forces. Although the activities of 'Dad's Army' are familiar today through the BBC TV comedy programme, much of the work undertaken by the battalion was far from funny. Seven members were killed by enemy action and sixty-three were injured. The Streatham Home Guard was the first unit in the country to be mentioned in despatches when Private P.D. Willeringhaus, a despatch rider, was cited for gallantry during an air raid.

Young men queue to enlist in the ARP in 1939. The Air Raid Wardens' Service was established in Streatham in 1938 and had a total of twenty-five posts situated throughout the area. About 1,000 wardens manned these posts day and night from the outbreak of war until December 1944 when the threat of bombing became negligible. As well as ensuring that the blackout rules were observed, a warden was appointed to direct the rescue work and supervise the Civil Defence units at the site of every bombing incident that occurred in Streatham.

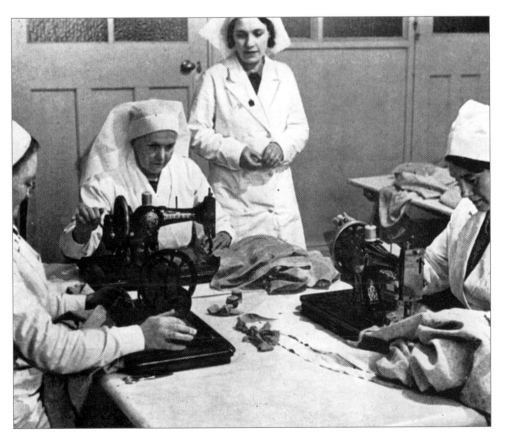

Volunteers working at the Streatham Hospital Supply Depot. Echoing the work of the War Hospital Supplies Depot established at Hill House in the First World War, a similar depot was set up in Leigham Court Road. This supplied hospitals and field stations with dressings and materials to treat both military and civilian casualties throughout the Second World War. Although much smaller than its predecessor, it still made a very valuable contribution to the war effort and over 100 women volunteers worked there.

Members of Streatham's Heavy Rescue Service with some of the Christmas toys they made for local children to replace those destroyed in the Blitz. The Heavy Rescue Service was responsible for freeing casualties and survivors from badly bombed properties. This was very dangerous work and the unit was staffed by expert builders and construction workers. The service was initially based at Streatham Ice Rink, and then Streatham Town Hall, before moving to Coventry Hall in late 1940 where it remained for the rest of the war.

A high-explosive bomb fell on Southcroft Road, midway between Mitcham Lane and Ribblesdale Road, on the night of 3 October 1940. A direct hit was suffered by no. 267, seen here, which destroyed the roof and blew out the windows. Surrounding properties were hit by the blast and experienced a similar fate. Fortunately there were no fatalities at the incident although, as can be seen, extensive damage was caused. The houses were subsequently demolished and rebuilt to the same design.

Gleneldon Road was one of the most heavily bombed streets in Streatham during the Blitz. On the evening of 5 November 1940 a high-explosive bomb fell on no. 179. Fortunately no one was seriously injured in the explosion but surrounding properties were badly damaged, as can be seen here when Civil Defence workers secured the premises the following morning. Seven other bombs fell in the road during the winter of 1940/1 of which three did not explode and had to be defused and made safe by members of the bomb disposal squad.

This was all that was left of 9 Stanthorpe Road after a high-explosive bomb fell here on the night of 29 October 1940. Miraculously the people sheltering in the house at the time were rescued unhurt, although the house was completely ruined. This picture shows the difficult circumstances under which the rescue services operated, particularly bearing in mind that much of their work was undertaken at night in almost complete darkness. The house and its neighbour at no. 7 were knocked down after the war and replaced with council flats.

Of the many fatal incidents in Streatham during the Blitz, one of the most tragic occurred on the night of 17 October 1940 when a high-explosive bomb fell on the Fire Station in Mitcham Lane. The bomb scored a direct hit on the firemen's quarters killing eleven firemen and seriously injuring three others. Seventy-year-old John Lynch was also killed in the incident. The station was so badly wrecked that the right-hand side of the building had to be knocked down and this photograph shows the work in progress.

The band of No. 6 Squadron of the Women's Junior Air Corps (WJAC) march down Mitcham Lane on church parade to St Leonard's Church in 1941. The squadron was established in March 1941 in response to requests from the Streatham League of Youth for a local organisation in which girls could serve. It was the first squadron to be set up in London and its drum and bugle band was the first girls' band of its type in England. It led 1,000 WJAC members in a marchpast in Regent Street where the salute was taken by HRH the Duchess of Kent. About 225 members of the Streatham WJAC joined the forces and 212 were subsequently involved in munitions or other forms of essential war work.

Lady Louis Mountbatten visits No. 5 First Aid Post in July 1941. The post was based at the Congregational Church, at Streatham Hill, and was mainly staffed by local members of the British Red Cross and the St John Ambulance Brigade. During the Blitz this post, together with Post No. 6 based at Streatham Baths, treated over 1,000 casualties as well as 760 victims of street accidents. During the war over 1,000 visits were made by staff to patients in their homes to relieve pressure on GPs and local medical services. During periods of inactivity staff from the post served in hospitals, clinics and nurseries.

During Warship Week in 1942 Wandsworth Borough set a target of raising a million pounds to adopt the anti-aircraft cruiser HMS *Cairo*. Streatham collected £367,309 and the borough easily surpassed its objective, raising £1.75 million. However, news that the vessel had been torpedoed while on convoy duty to Malta was a great blow to Wandsworth and to avenge this loss Streatham organised a special week in September in which every street in the neighbourhood was organised with a Savings Group. During this week local Scouts pulled a large model of the *Cairo*, seen above, throughout Streatham to help promote the campaign (see p. 61).

Streatham Forces Club, 1942. To provide recreational facilities for members of the armed forces in the area, a Streatham Forces Club was established by the Women's Voluntary Service in a large house in Woodbourne Avenue. The club was opened on 19 March 1942 by Sir Edward Grigg, a former Under Secretary of State for War, supported by Lord Nathan. The club provided a common room, men's lounge, writing room, card room, games room, bathroom, chapel and a girls' lounge with an adjoining bathroom. A small shop and cloakroom were constructed in the hallway.

Women of the National Fire Service on parade at the Regal Cinema (now the ABC) in Streatham as part of a local recruiting drive. The Auxiliary and Regular Fire Service, which combined in August 1942 to form the National Fire Service, did sterling work in Streatham throughout the war. In 1940–1 it attended 356 local fires caused by incendiaries, oil and high-explosive bombs dropped during the Blitz, as well as responding to the firebomb raids and the forty-one V1 flying bombs that fell in the locality during 1944.

On 13 June 1944 the
Archbishop of Canterbury,
Dr William Temple, seated
centre right, visited St Leonard's
Church as part of Streatham
churches 'Religion and Life'
week. The event commenced
with a rally on Streatham
Common attended by over
4,000 local residents. By sheer
coincidence the week saw the
beginning of the V1 attacks on
Streatham with the first bomb
falling on Friday 16 June. Over
the next two months 41 V1s
were to land in the area
claiming 86 lives and injuring
over 900 people as well as
causing considerable
devastation to local property.

A Civil Defence worker stands guard over bomb-shattered properties in Pathfield Road caused by the second V1 to fall on
Streatham. The explosion occurred at no. 23 at about midnight on 18 June 1944 and resulted in three residents losing their
lives: sisters Annie and Violet Potts at no. 23 and Kate Allsup at no. 22 who died later from her injuries in Wilson Hospital,
Mitcham. Casualties were high with about forty people being injured. Many properties had to be demolished and new houses
were erected on the site after the war.

A V1 did not have to score a direct hit to cause death and destruction as was the case at 6 p.m. on the evening of 22 June 1944 when a bomb fell into the River Graveney at the back of 48 Sherwood Avenue. Ten people were killed in neighbouring properties in Sherwood Avenue and Woodmansterne Road and there were over thirty serious casualties. Note the undamaged mirror on the first-floor bedroom wall which survived the blast although the house and surrounding properties were completely gutted.

Members of the Streatham Women's Voluntary Service (WVS) distribute furniture presented by people in the West Country to families whose possessions were lost in V1 explosions in 1944. Throughout the war the WVS provided the backbone of voluntary social work in the neighbourhood. It was active in running canteens, rest centres and the Forces Club, organising salvage collections and National Savings campaigns and providing practical help and assistance to the many thousands of local residents whose property was wrecked in the Blitz or during the V1 campaign in 1944.

One of the most destructive V1s to fall on Streatham exploded on the open ground at the junction of Sherwood Avenue and Glenister Park Road at 7 p.m. on the evening of 29 June 1944. Miraculously there were no serious casualties but the extent of damage caused was considerable, affecting houses as far afield as Woodmansterne Road and the other side of Hawkhurst Road. The photograph above shows the scale of the wreckage with rescue workers standing among the debris of the explosion. Roofs have been lifted, windows blown out and walls smashed. In the view below a doctor supervises the rescue of a man who was trapped in an Anderson Shelter located in a ground-floor room of his home. The house has been completely blown away leaving only the Anderson Shelter standing.

Hoadley Road was shaken at 10.30 on the morning of 30 June 1944 when a V1 exploded at no. 11. Miss McSweeney was fatally injured in the explosion and her pet Old English Sheepdog died in the blast. Here we can see members of the rescue services giving a trapped woman some water through a length of rubber tubing. On the right, a member of the Heavy Rescue Service considers the best way of releasing her safely from the surrounding debris.

At 7 a.m. on 3 July 1944 a V1 bomb smashed into the side of Streatham Hill Theatre, blowing out the wall of the building and destroying part of the circle balcony. Civil Defence parties were quick to arrive on the scene and rapidly set about rescuing members of staff and their friends who were asleep in the underground bars and lounges being used as shelters. Mrs Emma Jones, aged eighty-eight, was killed in the incident. The theatre was not repaired until well after the war and it did not open again until Boxing Day 1950.

Streatham High Road is covered with broken glass and rubble following the explosion of a V1 in the gardens of the Streatham War Memorial opposite at 2 p.m. on 5 July 1944. The bomb landed in a tree before falling onto the pavement below where it exploded, demolishing a police box and wardens' post. Amazingly the War Memorial was unharmed although the blast caused considerable damage to the shops and buildings on the western side of Streatham High Road, at the junction with Lewin Road. These properties were subsequently demolished and the land is one of the last remaining bomb sites in Streatham, currently occupied with advertising hoardings.

The resident of 140 Moyser Road peers out from the doorway of his garden shed, his temporary home after the blast of the V1 bomb falling nearby in the front garden of no. 144 destroyed his house. The explosion occurred at 5 a.m. on 21 July 1944 and resulted in the death of Warrant Officer Donald Alden and his wife, Muriel, at their home at 17 Furzedown Drive. This was an area that was badly hit by bombing during the war; a V1 claimed the lives of Alice Ramsden and Frank Corben at their homes at 30 and 36 Moyser Road, respectively, on the morning of 5 August 1944, and during the Blitz almost a dozen bombs fell in the neighbouring streets.

Extensive destruction was caused to the Streatham Hill High School for Girls by the V1 bomb that fell at the junction of Daysbrook and Wavertree Roads at midnight on 27 July 1944. Charles Kirby, an 84-year-old pensioner of 23 Wavertree Road, died in the explosion. The school continued at temporary premises at Herne Hill. After the war the old hall was enlarged and the new building was opened by HRH The Duchess of Gloucester on 22 October 1952. A plaque at the school commemorates the bombing.

Residents of Pendle Road were woken from their slumbers at 3 a.m. on 3 August 1944 when a V1 fell at the rear of nos 117–21. Twelve people lost their lives in this incident, including five women thought to have been either French or Belgian refugees who were living at no. 121. The WVS mobile canteen was soon on the scene and here we can see refreshments being served to naval ratings who helped the local Civil Defence services repair the wrecked properties.

Sir Gordon Hearn, founder-president of the Streatham Antiquarian and Natural History Society and chairman of the Streatham Ratepayers' Association, collects a war savings contribution from Alderman Mills and his wife. A Local Savings Committee was formed in Streatham in the early days of the war and its activities met with considerable success. It is estimated that more than £5 million was invested in National Savings in Streatham during the war, with Savings Groups formed in 16 schools, 82 businesses, 22 social clubs and 207 streets.

On 10 May 1945, two days after VE Day, HM King George VI and HM Queen Elizabeth, accompanied by the Princesses Elizabeth and Margaret, seen above, made an official visit to Streatham as part of their tour of some of the worst-bombed areas of London. Crowds ten deep lined the royal route, including some Italian prisoners of war whose transport had been delayed to allow the royal car to pass by. Thousands of children cheered as the royal party arrived at Sunnyhill Road School where they were greeted by Streatham's MP, David Robertson, and the Mayor of Wandsworth, Councillor William Bonney, who introduced them to members of the local Civil Defence services.

A Stand Down ceremony for the Civil Defence services was held at Mitcham Lane Drill Hall on 30 June 1945 when the groups were disbanded. Over 800 people attended the event to pay tribute to the work and courage of all those who had worked in the various branches of the service throughout the war. The highlight of the evening was a Civil Defence tableau (above) showing the men and women of the service performing their various duties. The display was arranged by H.L. Faulkner, a District Welfare Warden, and F.H. Matthews, Incident Officer at Warden Post I 80.

The children and residents of Sunnyhill and Angles Roads pose before tucking into a 'Victory Tea' to celebrate the end of the war in Europe in May 1945. Similar rejoicing took place in Streatham to mark VJ Day, when the war against Japan came to an end on 14 August that year. However, it was not until 8 June 1946 that Wandsworth Council organised a formal Victory Celebration on Streatham Common with a Drumhead Service, concerts, children's entertainments, games and races, a cricket match and evening dancing to music provided by the band of The Coldstream Guards.

Postwar Streatham

Prefabs in Sternhold Avenue. Streatham emerged from the war seriously scarred by the experience. An estimated 88 per cent of buildings had been destroyed or damaged by the bombing and it was to be a decade before much of the housing stock had been repaired or replaced. To provide emergency accommodation over 400 prefabricated temporary houses were erected on bomb sites and on the edges of Streatham and Tooting Bec Commons. Known as 'prefabs' some remained in existence for about forty years after the war had ended; those in Sternhold Avenue were still in use in the early 1980s.

In June 1946 Queen Mary visited the Darby and Joan Club in Streatham. The club was founded by Sir David Robertson, Streatham's MP, seated next to the Queen. The club was established to provide a social centre specifically designed to cater for the needs of elderly residents. It opened in December 1942 at Woodlawns, 16 Leigham Court Road, and continues to operate today at the same address providing the retired with companionship and a wide range of social activities.

Each Christmas since the war the Roman Catholic organisation the Knights of St Columba has placed a crib on Streatham Common. The Streatham branch was established in 1933 and is based at St Bartholomew's Church in Ellison Road. In 1985 Lambeth Council refused to have the crib on the Common claiming the Knights were not representative of local religious groups. Amid national headlines of 'Away with the Manger' the decision did much to accentuate the Labour council's 'Loony Left' image at the time. Today the crib continues to be a part of Streatham's Christmas celebrations and residents gather around it to sing carols.

Streatham High Road looking north from Gleneagle Road junction. A wet Wednesday afternoon in the late 1940s shows the street virtually deserted of shoppers. Wednesday was Streatham's traditional early closing day and most retailers would close at noon and take the afternoon off to compensate for having to work all day on Saturday. Local traders had little to be joyful about in the period immediately after the war; few residents had money to spend and few shops had a full range of goods to sell. Rationing remained in force well after hostilities ceased and was not completely abolished until 1954. The view below shows the same stretch of High Road from the top of the hill in the early 1950s. Note the motorbike and side car on the right which was a popular means of transport at the time. In those days riders were permitted to travel on a motorbike without having to wear a crash helmet.

Two trams are about to pass the dilapidated façade of the old Golden Domes Cinema near the High Road junction with Woodbourne Avenue in April 1948. The cinema opened in September 1912 with the screening of *Caesar Borgia*. The building could only seat 900 people and by the late 1930s was unable to compete with the larger and newer cinemas that had opened in Streatham. It closed in November 1938 and the building remained derelict until it was converted into a furniture store in 1955. It became a Tesco supermarket in 1968 and is now the Land of Leather furniture shop.

Almost 600 residents gather at the Locarno in October 1948 to celebrate the Golden Jubilee of the Streatham Chamber of Commerce. The event should have been held in 1947 but was delayed because of food restrictions that were then in force. The fiftieth anniversary dinner and dance was the social highlight of the year in Streatham and was described as 'without doubt the most brilliant event of its kind'. No fewer than four bands played throughout the evening and the speeches were recorded onto a gramophone record, copies of which were later sold at the local radio shop.

Compare these views of a bustling Streatham High Road in the early 1950s with that on the top of p. 65. Saturday was by far the busiest day for High Road traders and it was not uncommon for the pavement to be crowded with people doing their weekly shopping. A lack of traffic on the road meant people could cross the street and visit a variety of outlets without fear of being run down. With the exception of a handful of stores, most of the retailers were small independent traders, some of whom had been established in Streatham for many years. Tyrrell's the drapers, on the corner of the High Road and Prentis Road (below), was founded in 1886 and continued to trade in Streatham until 1968. On the right, at the junction of Shrubbery Road, is John Collier's, the 'Fifty Shilling Tailor', where a three-piece suit, comprising a jacket, trousers and a waistcoat, could be purchased for £2 10s (£2.50p).

A tram stands at the change-pit near the High Road junction with Gleneagle Road in February 1951. This is where power for the trams was switched from conduit lines to overhead wires. At the time this photograph was taken the days of the trams were numbered as they were being replaced with double-decker buses. Streatham's last tram trundled along the High Road on 7 April 1951 and the occasion was celebrated with much festivity tinged with sadness. One of the benefits of scrapping the trams was the removal of the unsightly overhead power lines that ran from the change-pit south to Norbury.

Sunnyhill Road School nativity play, 1952. Celestial angels surround the Three Wise Men, King Herod, Joseph, the Virgin Mary and the baby Jesus, with sundry shepherds and Roman soldiers looking on. The gathered throng is accompanied with 'heavenly music' provided by recorder players, one of whom is the actor, Hywel Bennett. He is seated in the second row, third from the right. Hywel made his first appearance on the stage as 'Doc' in the school's production of *Snow White and the Seven Dwarves* and went on to star in films and on television.

To celebrate Queen Elizabeth II's coronation in 1953 numerous street parties were held throughout Streatham. In Danbrook Road flags and bunting provided a festive backdrop for the high tea and party games held in the road. Here we see local children gathering around Cal McCord, the radio 'cowboy', ready to receive their prizes. Cal, dressed in his Stetson hat and cowboy boots, lived in nearby Fontaine Road and starred in a popular postwar Wild West radio programme. Cal was a well-liked local celebrity and was frequently seen riding his horse 'Ladybird' on Wimbledon Common.

Streatham Hill Station was the town's first railway station and was built by the West End of London & Crystal Palace Junction Railway. This photograph was taken about one-hundred years after the station was opened on 1 December 1856 and shows how little the building had changed in the intervening years. A poster outside the station advertises British Railways' cheap tickets. In 1953 a third-class return from Streatham Hill to Brighton cost 7s (35p) and, for those with more money to spare, a journey to Eastbourne and back could be obtained for 9s (45p).

The ladies of St Andrew's Women's Fellowship are assembled in the vicarage garden in Guildersfield Road in the mid-1950s for this photograph. The group was led by Miss Ruth Whittington, sitting sixth from the left. She and her sister lived in Braxted Park and were life-long supporters of St Andrew's Church. They were both teachers at Lexden House School which operated from 10 Heybridge Avenue until it closed in 1953. The Whittingtons were well known to local children and were easy to tell apart as Ruth always wore blue clothes while her sister, Ivy, dressed in brown.

Christ Church School pupils 'hit the bottle' in 1959. Headmaster Oliver Whyman discovered a novel and thrifty way of teaching music to his pupils in the 1950s using a collection of old beer and wine bottles. They were filled with varying amounts of water to produce a musical note when struck with a small wooden hammer. The Head kept beat with his baton and each child struck their bottle at the appropriate time to produce a tune. Port and sherry bottles were preferred for the middle notes, with a pint beer bottle best for a top A, while a quart cider flagon was ideal for a bottom A.

Streatham Common pond, *c.* 1959. The large number of young children in Streatham after the war meant that the paddling ponds on Streatham Common were always crowded throughout the summer months during the 1950s. The ponds were popular with parents as young children could enjoy the water in safety while their mothers had the opportunity to catch up on local news. The lower pond, seen here, was originally a natural water hole used by livestock grazing on the Common. Between the wars it was drained and replaced with a concrete paddling pool that continues in use today.

The ancient shops at 147–59 Streatham High Road, seen here in 1959, are among the oldest retail premises to survive in Streatham. Formerly known as Bedford Row, they were named after the Duke of Bedford, the Lord of the Manor of Streatham and Tooting Bec. They were originally small cottages, the ground floors being later converted into shops. No. 157, occupied by H.C. de Lacey, optician, was the birthplace of Major Frederick Henry Johnson who was awarded the Victoria Cross for his gallantry in France in 1915 (see p. 28).

The Chairman of the London County Council Education Committee, Mr H.C. Shearman, speaking at the presentation of the statue 'Lesson' to the Rosa Bassett School in Welham Road on 23 July 1959. The statue, of a naked mother and child, is by Franta Belsky. The school was named after its first headmistress, Miss Rosa Bassett, who served from 1906 to 1925. She pioneered the Dalton Plan of education based on the principle that children are eager to learn and should have freedom to make their own decisions and work at their own pace. The school buildings now form part of Graveney School.

Bishop Thomas Grant School, 1960. This school was built on farmland attached to St Michael's Convent, formerly known as Park Hill. It was designed by F. Broadbent and was opened in September 1959 by Archbishop Cyril Cowderoy. It was the largest secondary school in the diocese and at its peak accommodated 1,400 pupils. The school is named after Bishop Thomas Grant who was the first Roman Catholic Bishop of Southwark from 1851 to 1870. Note the castle tower at the rear of the school which was constructed in 1874 for the Leaf family of Park Hill as an ornamental garden feature or folly.

The Western Theatre Ballet at the Grass Theatre, Streatham Common, in July 1963. The small open-air theatre on Streatham Common was a popular venue for performances and was laid out at the top of the Common in the late 1930s. A wide variety of productions were staged here by a mixture of professional and amateur groups, ranging from the Morley College Actors who staged Shakespeare's *Comedy of Errors* here in July 1952, to the Imperial Opera Company who appeared in 1961 with their production of *The Marriage of Figaro*.

This row of small shops stood opposite Streatham Common from at least the early 1700s. The buildings were constructed from old ships' timbers with the walls and ceilings being plastered using mud and horse hair. The Adams family established their sports and travel goods shop here in 1883 and continued to trade until these properties were demolished in the 1960s to make way for an extension to the adjacent P.B. Cow's India rubber factory. Note York Cottage; when it was pulled down Streatham lost one of its last 'Dainty Tea' shops.

Opening of new classrooms at Christ Church School, Streatham Hill, 1964. By the mid-1960s facilities at Christ Church School were seriously stretched with cramped and crowded classrooms and only 4 washbasins to serve 200 pupils. To relieve this pressure new facilities were constructed at the rear of the school on part of the playground. Here we see the Bishop of Southwark blessing one of the two new classrooms. The extension was formerly declared open on 9 June by the head boy and head girl of the school, Stephen Clapham and Annette Scriven.

Nos 289–91 Streatham High Road. This pair of grand, semi-detached Victorian houses stood on the northern junction of the High Road and Baldry Gardens. In 1913 D.C. Goodswin moved to no. 291. He was an early cinema pioneer and a director of Modern Picture Playhouses Ltd. Note the small top-floor rooms that were used to accommodate the domestic servants employed here. By the 1960s these houses had a somewhat dilapidated and rundown appearance and they were demolished and replaced with a block of flats.

The old metal emblem of a White Lion and a
Watneys Red Barrel lamp hang over the entrance to
the White Lion public house in Streatham High Road
in the 1960s. Pints have been quaffed in an inn on
this site since at least 1507 when Henry Knight
owned the premises. The sign was erected when the
old pub was rebuilt by Purchase and Perham in
1895. A large stone lion used to stand on the roof of
the old inn and was a well-known local landmark. In
June 1997 the pub was refurbished and reopened as
the Hobgoblin.

By the late 1960s the High Road was beginning to change and many of the old prewar shop fronts were
being replaced with modern façades. Here we see the traditional frontage of Cordeau's delicatessen alongside
the more streamlined design of The National Bank. Cordeau's was one of Streatham's oldest traders having
been established by Arthur Cordeau in 1920. After his death in 1967 the business was run by his son, also
Arthur. The shop specialised in food cooked on the premises in the traditional French style.

Derwent's television shop occupied nos 15 and 16 Leigham Hall Parade in Leigham Avenue. By the late 1960s watching television was Britain's most popular pastime. Most homes in Streatham had a 'telly' in the corner of their living room and Derwent's were able to offer the latest models from as little as £15. Clients could either pay for sets outright or buy them on hire purchase. For those concerned that the TV set would not blend in with their decor Derwent's provided a range of reproduction cabinets in which the set could be placed and concealed from view when not in use.

A few traditional laundries still survived in Streatham in the 1960s, although by this time coin-operated launderettes were becoming increasingly popular. The Sunlight Laundry and Dry Cleaners was situated at 111 Mitcham Lane, on the northern junction with Westcote Road. It was established a few years before the Second World War in an old furniture shop, in premises that had formerly been known as Skelder House.

The Dutch Boy Garage, 10 Sternhold Avenue, not far from Streatham Hill. It was established in 1928 by John Austen Sparks who set up a small garage and motor repair shop here which was to grow into a large engineering company with works in nearby Ardwell Road and in Cardiff. In 1938 Sparks constructed the garage building seen in this late 1960s photograph. It was designed by the local architect Carl Remnant and survived until 1984 when it was demolished. Wentworth House, the Brixton South Jobcentre, now occupies the site.

The Temperance Billiard Hall is on the left of this view of Streatham High Road in the early 1960s. It was erected in 1928 and many locals have whiled away a misspent youth playing on its tables. By the mid-1960s players were no longer satisfied with the amenities offered and Mecca completely refurbished the hall, reopening it in November 1965 as The Golden Q. One of the biggest attractions at the new club was not the seventeen gold baize-covered snooker tables but the one-arm bandit machines which led Mecca subsequently to convert the premises to a gambling club.

The Streatham Well House in Valley Road still retained much of its rural charm in the 1960s. The original spring was discovered in 1659 on a field adjacent to Streatham Common (see p. 16). When this well became contaminated in the 1790s the spa was transferred to a new spring discovered here. The Well House later became part of the Curtis Brothers Dairy which delivered the mineral waters with their milk until the Second World War when the well was closed due to bomb damage. The Spa House survives today amid a development of sheltered housing built on the surrounding land.

The South Metropolitan Gas Company moved to their new premises at 5–7 Streatleigh Parade, at the junction of Streatham High Road and Leigham Court Road, in January 1938. By the 1960s the company had become the South Eastern Gas Board and a large range of gas appliances were on view at their showroom. At this time salesmen were extolling the benefits of 'High Speed Gas' to Streatham housewives. The showroom continued to operate from this site until falling sales resulted in its closure by British Gas in August 1993. Note the fine development of Streatleigh Court flats above the shops.

The 1970s and '80s

Streatham High Road, 1973. Throughout the 1970s and 1980s the population of Streatham underwent a steady change. Larger properties continued to be converted into flats or bedsits leading to a steady increase in the number of younger residents. There was also a greater diversity in the ethnic mix of the local population. As a result, some of the town's long-established shops closed to be replaced by new supermarkets, boutiques and outlets catering for a younger clientele. As older residents died or moved away many of the local organisations found their numbers in decline as a new generation of residents preferred alternative activities.

This view of Palace Road in 1972 shows the large barrier that used to completely block the entrance to the street from Christchurch Road. A large notice nearby informed travellers that it was a private road and prohibited its use by 'Heavy Traffic, Funerals & Hawkers'. Palace Road was developed as part of the Roupell Park Estate. It is named after the Crystal Palace which moved to nearby Sydenham in 1854 after housing the Great Exhibition in Hyde Park in 1851.

Two 'totters' pass St James's Mission Hall, in Eardley Road, on their horse-drawn rag-and-bone cart in 1972. The hall dates from the early 1890s and was erected here by Immanuel Church for the inhabitants of West Streatham. The hall has seen a variety of uses over the years and has been home to the Streatham Boys' Club and the British Legion. It is now occupied by IBA Interiors Ltd. On the embankment, behind the hall, stands the Streatham Junction South railway signal-box, replacing an earlier box here which ceased operations in October 1952.

The original entrance to Streatham Station was situated in Streatham Station Approach, seen above, in 1979. The station was opened by the South London and Sutton Junction Railway in 1868. Passengers wishing to cross the line were forced to use a wooden footbridge which drew considerable criticism from travellers. As traffic increased it was decided to construct a new station and the building seen below in 1972 was constructed on the bridge over the railway lines in 1898. This enabled passengers to gain access to both platforms from the booking hall without having to use the footbridge, which was removed. The new building also provided the station with a prestigious new entrance which was considered more in keeping with Streatham's growing importance as a select residential area. This building served local commuters until 1991 when a new station was opened here.

Streatham Town Hall was built in 1887 to provide a venue for concerts, lectures and public meetings. The opening night concert was a great success and concluded with Sims Reeves, a popular tenor of the day, singing 'Come Into the Garden Maud' to rapturous applause. This view shows the main hall in Gleneagle Road shortly before it was demolished in 1973. The High Road entrance was pulled down in 1988. The site was to be developed as Streatham's new police station but due to a lack of funds it is now earmarked for commercial development as housing and shops.

Sideburns and long hair were much in vogue when this photograph of Ronnie's hairdressers in Leigham Avenue was taken in 1972. The salon was established in 1952 by Ronnie Lees Smith who used to give customers a pint of beer with their haircut at Christmas. In 1954 the comedy actor Peter Sellers helped pour the first yuletide pint. Peter declined a haircut but instead asked that Ronnie trim the coats of his two dogs! The salon was later owned by Michael Travers who was an actor and songwriter. He produced tunes for Edmundo Ross and Billy Cotton, and in the 1970s appeared in BBC TV productions of *Anna Karenina* and *War and Peace*.

The Rookery had been a centre of peace and tranquillity in Streatham until the night of 31 March 1973 when vandals devastated the gardens. Seats were ripped up and thrown into the goldfish pond; rustic trellis was torn from the walls; five 7 ft high stone pillars were toppled over and a 50 yd length of a garden wall was broken down; trees were uprooted and flower beds and lawns were laid waste. It took many months of hard labour for staff to restore the gardens to their former glory, as seen in this view taken after the work was completed.

The 'old crocks' drive past Streatham Hill Station on the London to Brighton Veteran Car run in 1974. This popular annual event normally attracts large numbers of residents who line the High Road between 8 and 10 a.m. on the first Sunday in November to cheer on the vintage cars as they pass by on their 50-mile drive to the coast. The first run took place in 1896 to celebrate the Act of Parliament that removed the need for a man to walk 20 yd in front of a mechanical vehicle and set the future speed limit of 12mph at which motor cars could travel.

On the night of 5 May 1975 a fire completely gutted Streatham's ancient parish church of St Leonard's. Despite firemen fighting the blaze well into the early hours of the morning all that was left standing was the tower and outer walls of the building. From these remains a new church was built to the designs of local architects the Douglas Feast Partnership. The new church was rededicated by the Bishop of Southwark on 22 December 1976. In 1999 the final phase of the rebuilding project was completed when the churchyard was landscaped and railings placed around its perimeter.

Pupils at Julian's Primary School in Leigham Court Road enjoy a pony cart ride at their Summer Fête in the mid-1970s. The school was built in 1968 to replace the nearby Crown Lane Primary School. The opening of the new school was delayed and construction work was not completed when the first pupils arrived in September. The school originally comprised 5 classrooms which could accommodate 280 children. It is built partly on the site of allotments that used to cover wasteland at the rear of Leigham Court Road.

Queen Elizabeth II's Silver Jubilee celebrations, Lewin Road, 1977. Children in Lewin Road decorated their bicycles with Union flags, tinsel and ribbons to celebrate the first twenty-five years of the Queen's reign. Throughout Streatham various street parties were organised and many of the roads were bedecked with bunting and flags to mark the occasion. At St Leonard's School staff and pupils dressed in red, white and blue for the Jubilee school party. After an afternoon of games and races, a 'weeping' silver birch tree was planted in the school grounds to commemorate the day.

Local Cubs and Scouts parade down Garrads Road on their way to the St George's Day service at St Leonard's Church in the Queen's Silver Jubilee year of 1977. The 1st Streatham Scout Group hosted the parade. The group was formed in 1908 and is one of the oldest troops in existence. Sadly, the Chairman of St Leonard's Scout Group, George Wooster, died suddenly at his home in Hillcote Avenue in January 1977. George had been associated with the Streatham Scouts for thirty-two years and in 1976 was awarded the Medal of Merit for his services to Scouting.

Immanuel School, 1977. The original Immanuel School was situated in Factory Square opposite Streatham Common. It was built in 1861 to the designs of the architect George Gilbert Scott RA. The school was erected next to the P.B. Cow India rubber factory and over the years as the firm expanded the school gradually became surrounded by the works (see p. 94). In the 1970s serious concern arose over the risks this posed should there be a fire at the factory as there was only one way in and out of the site. The church, parents, school managers and staff mounted a successful campaign for the authorities to rebuild the school in nearby

Northanger Road. The new building was opened on 3 February 1977 by the Bishop of Kingston, Hugh Montefiore. The photograph on the left shows pupils at the new school recovering from a day 'clowning about' in fancy dress in the mid-1980s. The ground on which the old school stood is now covered by a Sainsbury's supermarket.

To celebrate the fiftieth anniversary of the Streatham Hill Theatre in 1978, the Streatham Society held a party at Streatham Baths. The guest of honour was the popular musical comedy actress Evelyn Laye (centre), who laid the foundation stone of the theatre on 6 September 1928. She later presented the society with the trowel she used on that occasion. Also present was Reg Exton (right), editor of the *Streatham News*, and Charles Chaperlin (left), who was appointed manager of the Locarno Ballroom in 1938 and opened two nightclubs in Streatham, the Stork Club in 1948 and the Peacock Club in 1964.

Standing at the top of Wellfield Road is Blackwood Hall, seen here in a derelict condition in the late 1970s. Formerly known as the Streatham Mission Hall, it was built in 1867 by Sir Arthur Blackwood who lived at Wood Lodge, a large house at the corner of Tooting Bec Road and Garrads Road. The Mission met with considerable success and in 1874 Sir Arthur founded the Trinity Presbyterian Church in Pendennis Road, and the hall was handed over to them for their use. Since 1995 the building has been used by the Bright Sparks Theatre School.

Cynthia Payne hit the headlines in 1978 when police raided her home in Ambleside Avenue and discovered a sex party in progress. At these gatherings men, including MPs, vicars and lawyers, exchanged 'luncheon vouchers' for food, drink and female companionship. The 1980 court case caused a sensation and Cynthia was sentenced to eighteen months' imprisonment for running a brothel. This was later reduced to six months on appeal. Fame followed, with books and two films based on her life: *Personal Services* staring Julie Walters and *Wish You Were Here* with Emily Lloyd. In 1988 Cynthia and 'Lord' David Sutch (below) formed the

Rainbow Alliance in the Kensington by-election, Cynthia standing for the Payne and Pleasure Party and Sutch for the Monster Raving Looney Party. 'Lord' Sutch lodged at Ambleside Avenue for most of 1988. Today Cynthia is a celebrity and a popular after-dinner speaker, winning the title of the 'Ideal Dinner Guest' on the BBC *Good Food Show*.

The Leigham Vale Morris Men celebrate May Day at the Leigham Arms, at the junction of Sunnyhill and Wellfield Roads, 1979. The group was founded in 1975 to maintain the spirit of traditional English dancing and to earn themselves free beer at the pubs where they dance. However, the group also performs for charity, on which occasions they buy their own ale! Bedecked in brightly coloured sashes, with bells dangling from their knees and carrying large handkerchiefs to ward off evil spirits, they tour pubs and village greens throughout south London keeping alive this ancient rural tradition.

The *Streatham News* office in Gleneldon Road decorated for the marriage of the Prince of Wales to Lady Diana Spencer in 1981. The first issue of the *Streatham News* was published on 18 July 1891 and sold for 1*d* a copy. The newspaper's office was originally based in Streatham High Road but moved to 1 Gleneldon Road in 1914 where it remained until 1985. The introduction of free local newspapers in the 1980s badly hit the circulation of the *Streatham News* and it converted to a 'free sheet' in 1985. The paper survives today as the *Streatham Mercury* published by South London Press.

89

Coventry Hall stood amid the large blocks of council flats in Albert Carr Gardens, between Streatham Common North and Hopton Road. The Hall was built in the early 1800s by Viscount Deerhurst, later to become the 7th Earl of Coventry, who purchased the old Streatham Manor House in 1798, which had stood here from at least Tudor times. In 1895 the Hall became a convent and the nuns established the St Andrew's Girls' School here. The property was requisitioned in the Second World War after which it was converted into flats by Wandsworth Council. Coventry Hall was demolished in 1982 and sheltered housing for the elderly was erected on the site in 1995 (see p. 103).

Century House was built in 1938 as the head office of James Walker jewellers. Sidney Sanders opened his first shop in Streatham in 1902 and quickly built up a chain of outlets. On entering into partnership with the James Walker business of Peckham, he adopted the latter name for the firm as it had been in existence since 1823, meaning the enlarged enterprise could claim to have been established from that date. At its peak James Walker traded from 127 outlets. Following the takeover of the business by Hill Samuel, Century House closed on 28 September 1984 and was subsequently converted into flats.

This row of single-storey lock-up shops, between Streatham Station and Station Approach, was demolished in 1984 to make way for a Safeway supermarket. It was the first of the purpose-built new superstores to be erected in Streatham and was opened on 4 December 1984. Safeway is one of the largest supermarkets in the area with 43,875 square feet of floor space and an extensive underground car park. Note on the right Gadsby's art shop which traded in Streatham for fifty years from 1946 to 1996. It is now a charity shop run by the local Spires Centre for the homeless (see p. 109).

Streatham Bus Garage was built by the London General Omnibus Company Ltd in 1913. It replaced a large detached house called Holmfield that had formerly been the boyhood home of Sir George Faudel Phillips, Lord Mayor of London between 1865 and 1866. The garage was demolished in 1986 and rebuilt at a cost of £4.5 million. This opened in February 1987 and accommodated 83 buses, plus minibuses and training vehicles, but subsequently closed in March 1992 with the loss of 200 jobs. The premises are now used as a Playscape Go-Kart track (see p. 104).

The first Mela Festival of Asian Culture was held in the Rookery Gardens in 1987. This photograph of the occasion shows an Indian dancer performing before a predominantly local audience. However, this annual event held during the August Bank Holiday weekend quickly grew in popularity attracting thousands of people from near and far. By 1992 it was pulling in such big crowds that it was moved to a larger arena on Streatham Common. After a record 12,000 visitors in 1996 Lambeth Council was forced to cease funding the event due to budgetary constraints and the Mela moved to Norbury Park.

One of the tallest trees on Streatham Common, a white poplar, was reduced to a 10 ft stump following the great storm that swept through southern England on the night of 16 October 1987. Residents woke that morning to find their cars trapped beneath fallen trees and everywhere roads were strewn with debris. Tiles had been torn from roofs and garden fences and sheds shattered by broken branches or blown down by the wind. That night gusts of up to 120mph had left a trail of death and destruction in its wake throughout England leaving 19 people dead and an estimated 15 million trees damaged or destroyed.

A thick layer of snow covers Southcroft Road in the late 1980s. This photograph is remarkable in that it was taken by Leslie Jarrett who was blind. A keen photographer, Leslie took this snap from the doorway of his home using a special camera. Despite his blindness Leslie led a full and active life. As well as his interest in photography he was also a keen bowler and played with other blind and partially sighted players whose bowls were guided towards the jack with the aid of directions from a fully sighted person.

The statue of John the Baptist looks out over Streatham Common from its vantage point on top of the drinking fountain of Immanuel Church. This photograph was taken shortly before the main body of the church was demolished in 1987 to make way for St John's House, providing sheltered accommodation for the elderly. The first Immanuel Church was erected in 1854 and was replaced in 1865 with the church we see here. Today all that remains of this building is the tower, behind which is a new church dedicated by the Bishop of Southwark, Ronald Bowlby, on 16 October 1988.

This photograph from the mid-1980s of part of P.B. Cow's factory complex was taken from the tower of Immanuel Church. P.B. Cow was one of Streatham's largest businesses and produced a range of rubber products. The company came to Streatham in 1851 when it took over the Forster and Carpenter works which was based in a Georgian silk mill; this can be seen in front of the chimney. The mill survives today as a Grade II listed building and houses a coffee shop and offices for the Sainsbury supermarket now occupying the site.

P.B. Cow flourished in Streatham, and additional buildings were put up on the site to accommodate the extra machinery needed to meet the rapidly rising demand for the company's rubber products. By the mid-1890s the workforce had grown to about 500, and P.B. Cow had firmly consolidated its position as the main employer in the area.

During the Second World War, the factory converted to war work, making 'Mae Wests', inflatable rubber dinghies, gas masks and other items. Two high-explosive bombs fell here in 1940 but it was an unexploded bomb that was discovered on the site on 11 January 1941 that had a more serious impact on production as staff were not allowed into the factory until it had been defused. After the war P.B. Cow resumed production of its peacetime products, including their famous 'Li-Lo' air beds.

In 1986 the factory complex was acquired by Sainsbury's who built a large supermarket on the site, opened by Lord Sainsbury on 21 November 1989.

Note Immanuel School in the middle of the site.

Towards the
New Millennium

Keith Hill celebrates becoming Streatham's first Labour MP in the 1992 General Election. To the left stands Sir William Shelton, the previous Conservative MP, and Cynthia Payne who stood for the Payne and Pleasure Party (see p. 88). The 1990s was a decade of change for Streatham. In 1990 the closure of Pratts, Streatham's largest store, began a period of decline with at one time almost a fifth of the shops in the High Road standing empty. However, by the end of the decade there had been a steady improvement in the town's fortunes and, with a new Sainsbury's convenience store set to open, local traders could look to the future with more confidence.

Pratts Department Store. For many residents the closure of Pratts in 1990 marked a bleak period in Streatham's fortunes. The store was established by George Pratt who came to Streatham in 1840 as a thirteen-year-old apprentice draper. He worked for William Reynolds in a small shop in Bedford Row, a terrace of small cottage properties opposite Streatham Green. When Reynolds retired George purchased the business and quickly increased trade. In 1867 he built Eldon House, seen above, from where his business continued to flourish. He later acquired large landholdings in Streatham and went on to develop the Bedford Park Estate. In 1885 George divided his business among his three sons and his department store was eventually acquired by the John Lewis Partnership. The company decided to close the store in 1990 and the building was demolished five years later. In 1996 a Lidl Super-market, an Argos store and sundry retail outlets opened on the site (left).

In the run-up to the 1992 General Election Streatham's Conservative MP, Sir William Shelton (second from left), and his Labour Party challenger, Keith Hill (third from right), don Streatham Against Litter T-shirts and help clean up the High Road. Ever since Streatham first elected its own Member of Parliament in 1918 the constituency had always returned a

Conservative MP. This long-standing tradition came to an end in the April 1992 General Election when Keith Hill turned Sir William Shelton's 2,407 majority into a Labour lead of 2,317 votes. Gracious in defeat, Sir William said he was sad to have lost the election, but if he had to lose his seat he preferred it to be to his friend Mr Hill. A number of senior politicians visited the constituency during the 1992 campaign, including the Prime Minister, Margaret Thatcher, and Denis Healey, seen right, talking to Brenda Hargreaves during his visit to the Megabowl at Streatham Hill.

By the early 1990s La Pergola and a neighbouring restaurant in Streatham High Road called Il Carretto had competed for business for thirteen years. It was then that their rivalry reached new heights when they both started to feature Elvis Presley impersonators to serenade their customers. For seven years diners were never lonesome at night with a choice of Elvis performers just two doors apart. In 1997 Kim Bridges at La Pergola became the unrivalled 'King' of the Streatham Presleys when the Il Carretto was sold and became the Hogshead pub.

The Megabowl, Streatham Hill. The Megabowl began life as the Gaumont Picture Palace (see p. 40) which was converted into the Streatham Bowl, Europe's largest bowling alley which opened on 29 January 1962. Top Rank sold the business to Mecca in 1967 who operated it until 1986 when the building closed. Following a major refurbishment by Allied Restaurants, it reopened as the 36-lane 'Megabowl' on 15 December 1989. Prince William and Prince Harry made two visits to the 'Zapp Zone' at the Megabowl in October 1992 when they had a hi-tech laser-gun duel with their detectives.

In 1992 Roe Bridge in Mitcham Lane was rebuilt. The bridge dates from the sixteenth century when Thomas Roe almost drowned when he was crossing the River Graveney. As a result he paid for a bridge to be built here. He was later knighted, was Master of the Merchant Taylors' Company in 1557 and became Lord Mayor of London in 1568. His bridge was renewed in 1652, incorporating this stone on which is carved the coat of arms of the Company, the date 1652 and the inscription 'This Bridge was made at the cost of the WORSHIPFUL COMPANY OF MERCHANT TAYLORS'. The bridge was rebuilt in 1772, 1906 and again in 1992, on each occasion the old memorial stone being incorporated into the structure.

Brixton Hill United Reform Church was built in 1993. A place of worship has stood on this spot at the top of Streatham Hill since 1829 when a Union Chapel was established here for use by Anglicans and Non-conformists living in this part of Streatham parish. The Anglicans left to form Christ Church in 1837 and the Baptists departed in 1842 to form their own congregation in New Park Road. The chapel then became a Congregational Church and was replaced with a new building in 1871. That church was demolished in 1982 and a new place of worship, seen here, was subsequently erected on the site in 1993.

Charlie Adams, Regional Director of the Housing Corporation (left), and Aman Dalvi, Chief Executive of the Ujima Housing Association (right), at the opening of new accommodation at 85–95 Sternhold Avenue in 1993. Ujima was established in 1977 to provide accommodation for young, black, single homeless people. It is now a general housing association providing affordable housing for those in need, the elderly and those requiring mental care. The Association also has properties at 69–79 Sunnyhill Road. Ujima is a Swahili word meaning Working Together.

In November 1993 the comedy actress June Whitfield, star of the BBC TV series *Absolutely Fabulous* and the *News Huddlines* on BBC Radio 2, attended the Christmas Bazaar at the Streatham Youth Club in Conyers Road. June, who spent her childhood in Streatham, helped out with the auction as well as drawing raffle tickets at the event. The club raised almost £2,000 for their annual Christmas party for over a hundred local youngsters. The Streatham Youth Club was founded in 1946 by John Corfield who was awarded the MBE in 1990 for his youth work.

Dennis and Jean Hembry at St Leonard's 1993 Christmas Bazaar. Jean was popularly known as Streatham's 'Cracker Lady' because of the artistic hand-made Christmas crackers she produced. In the Second World War she toured the world entertaining the troops and in 1991 wrote a book about her wartime experiences with the Entertainments National Service Association (ENSA). Jean continued to perform after the war, appearing in cabaret, revues and pantomime, and was a keen member of the Streatham Society Players. She died in 1998 aged seventy-nine.

Thames Water Pumping Station, Conyers Road. Often mistaken for a mosque, the Pumping Station is one of the architectural delights of Streatham. Built by the Southwark and Vauxhall Water Company in 1894, the 1,400 ft deep well used to supply 1.5 million gallons of water a day to local consumers. One-hundred years after the station was built it received a new lease of life when in 1994 the London Ring Main was completed and the works became one of eleven pumping stations which help circulate 285 million gallons of water a day around the 50-mile-long main to London residents.

In 1995 Caesars Night Club opened in the old Locarno Dance Hall (see p. 36). The Locarno had been relaunched several times in the past thirty years becoming the 'Cats Whiskers' in 1969, 'The Studio' in 1984 and 'The Ritzy' in 1990. Caesars is modelled on a Roman theme and has proved a popular venue for revellers. It currently holds disco nights on Thursdays with club nights on Fridays and Saturdays. Britain's first professional female boxing bout took place here in November 1998 when Jane Couch, the 'Fleetwood Assassin', beat Semon Lukic of Germany.

The 1995 Garden Open Day at the residence of Cllr Brian Palmer in Woodbourne Avenue. Since 1995 Mr Palmer, a garden designer, has opened his garden to the public under the National Gardens Scheme with proceeds being donated to charity. The garden is one of the finest in Streatham and has featured in Sainsbury's magazine and other publications. The front garden is laid out as a cottage garden with roses, irises and herbaceous plants, with the rear area designed as a country garden with shrubs, trees, a gazebo and a pool, creating a tranquil oasis in an urban setting.

New life came to St Andrew's Church Hall at the southern end of Colmer Road in 1995 when it was completely renovated and converted into the Shree Swaminarayan Temple. Most of the conversion work was undertaken by members of the temple themselves who raised more than £50,000 to buy the raw materials required. A week-long festival marked the opening of the temple. The building dates from 1869 and was originally an infant school. It was designed by the local architect, Sir Ernest George, and is believed to be the earliest known example of his work.

In 1995 a new development of sheltered housing was erected on the site of Coventry Hall, near Streatham Common (see p. 90). The twenty-four units occupy the land on which the 7th Earl of Coventry's mansion once stood. The homes were specially designed for elderly people and were opened by the TV comedy actress Angela Thorne of the BBC series *To The Manor Born* and *Three Up, Two Down*. The new accommodation, also known as Coventry Hall, was developed in consultation with residents in neighbouring sheltered housing as the new building also provides them, as well as its new occupants, with communal facilities.

For the first time since the Second World War Streatham was lit up for Christmas in 1995 when Lambeth Council placed illuminations on the lamp-posts along Streatham High Road. The local actress Linda Baron, who played the part of Nurse Gladys Immanuel in the popular BBC TV series *Open All Hours*, switched on the lights outside the Odeon Cinema. The large crowd gathered for the occasion was entertained by the choir of Sunnyhill Road School and the steel band from Immanuel School. Standing opposite Linda is Lambeth's Town Crier, Alfie Howard, who officiated at the proceedings.

In 1996 Playscape Pro Racing Ltd opened the Streatham Kart Raceway in Streatham Bus Garage which had remained unused since it closed in 1992. The company laid out an indoor go-kart track in the garage, providing a 400 m long circuit for the forty karts that are based here. With fifteen heated pit bays for team racing Streatham provides a popular venue for corporate hospitality. Playscape was established in a car park in 1989 by Martin Howell, who has since seen the £2,000 redundancy money he sunk into the enterprise grow into a £1.5 million a year business.

Swallow Gardens, Mitcham Lane, was built in 1996 and is a small development of two- and three-bedroom houses on the site of the old Territorial Army base later used by British Telecom. The houses either side of the entrance in Mitcham Lane and to the rear in Babington Road, were erected by the Tower Housing Association to provide affordable accommodation. They were offered for sale on a shared ownership basis with a 50 per cent interest in a two-bedroom house being initially available at a cost of £35,000.

In 1997 Brian Fraser purchased the Bingo Hall established by Mecca in the Streatham Hill Theatre after it closed in 1962 (see p. 36). Brian, who had previously worked as a regional manager for Mecca Bingo, renamed the hall Mayfair Bingo and in its first two years of operation under his management visitor numbers have more than doubled to 3,500 a week. Players have done well at the club and in 1999 two people each won £100,000 in a single night. The building is considered an outstanding example of interwar theatre architecture and is Grade II listed.

Barry McGuigan, the former world featherweight boxing champion, visited Streatham in February 1997 to open O'Neill's pub at 78 Streatham High Road. The opening night was a great success with all the Guinness poured that evening having a shamrock design on the head. The pub creates the image of an old Irish country store at the turn of the century. Although the front of the building looks as if it has graced the High Road since Victorian times, it only dates from 1997 and replaced the modern façade of a pizza restaurant which previously occupied part of these premises. This pub now trades as Taylors.

The Mayor of Lambeth, Nick Cattermole (right), and Streatham's MP, Keith Hill (left), launch Streatham Against Litter's can recycling campaign on Streatham Common in July 1997. The project was aimed at encouraging people to separate their aluminium drinks cans from other waste so they could be recycled, and at the same time help make the Common a tidier place. The Streatham scheme is one of seven similar campaigns in Lambeth. Money raised from the sale of the aluminium waste is used to fund improvements in Lambeth's parks and commons.

The Holland Tringham pub in Streatham High Road opened in December 1998 and is named after a local artist. Examples of his work hang on the pub's walls depicting views of Streatham in the nineteenth century. Joseph Holland Tringham was born in Hammersmith in 1861 and came to live in Streatham in 1891 when he was at the height of his skills, working for such magazines as the *Graphic* and the *Illustrated London News*. Sadly, a series of family tragedies led him into drunkenness and his health slowly declined. He died in a lunatic asylum on the Isle of Man in March 1908 aged forty-six.

With so much traffic on Streatham's roads it is not too surprising to find a car parked on a roof! Such is the case at Gasoline Alley, at 50 Streatham High Road, where a plastic and fibreglass replica of a 1950s red Cadillac sits atop this car accessory shop. The store was opened in March 1998 by the 'Page Three' model Jo Guest. The shop is dedicated to the memory of James Dean and a clock is mounted in the roof rafters showing the time of his death – 5.59 p.m. on 30 December 1955. The inside of the store is decorated with 1950s memorabilia including original gas pumps and a telephone of the period. The building was originally the Temperance Billiard Hall (see p. 77).

In the early hours of the morning of 10 March 1992 fire completely gutted St Andrew's Church in Guildersfield Road. Designed by the local architect Sir Ernest George, the church was built in 1886 as a memorial to the Revd Stenton Eardley, the first vicar of Immanuel Church. Although St Andrew's was a Grade II listed building, the damage caused by the fire made the structure unsafe and the church was pulled down. The photograph shows demolition work in progress in June 1994. A new vicarage for Immanuel Church was erected on part of the plot and stands adjacent to the old St Andrew's vicarage which is now a private residence. Graveney Villas (below), a terrace of five houses, has occupied the remainder of the site since 1999. A novel design feature of these houses is that the middle three dwellings have an additional bedroom concealed in the roof.

One of Streatham's last housing developments of the twentieth century was Park Gate in Garrads Road. The large Victorian house at the centre of the site was originally the home of Jane Fisher, daughter of Beriah Drew, Lord of the Manor of Leigham. In 1880 the house became the Elms School and from about 1910 it was used as St John the Baptist's Nursery Home. In the 1960s Lambeth Council developed the property as a residential home for the elderly, opened in September 1966 by Mrs Harold Wilson, the Prime Minister's wife. The council sold the property in 1997 and the buildings in the grounds were demolished to make way for the Park Gate Estate.

Lunchtime at the Spires Centre in 1999. The Centre was founded in 1990 to provide meals for local homeless people over Christmas. From this humble beginning a day centre has been established at St Leonard's Church Hall providing essential services to hundreds of disadvantaged members of the local community. Volunteers currently prepare over 8,000 hot meals a year at the centre and tons of second-hand clothing is processed and made available to clients. The centre also operates a resettlement scheme, a primary healthcare clinic, and an alcohol and drugs advisory service.

The spire and steeple of Streatham's parish church of St Leonard's has long been a prominent landmark at the heart of the town. A church has occupied this spot for at least a thousand years and a chapel is recorded here in the Domesday Book of 1086. Streatham's history can be traced back to Roman times and artefacts from this period have been unearthed in the parish churchyard. The tower is the oldest part of the church and dates from the mid-thirteenth century when the church is believed to have been rebuilt by Sir John Ward whose effigy survives behind the altar.

Children stand at the junction of Mitcham Lane and Greyswood Street in 1913.

Acknowledgements and Picture Credits

Our thanks go to the following for the use of their photographs. (Page no. t = top, b = bottom):

Elizabeth Barrett 72t, 93t, 102b, 104b, rear endpaper
Brian Bloice 48b, 49b, 50t, 51tb, 52t, 53tb, 54tb, 55t, 56b, 58b, 61b
John Brown viii, 6t, 17, 18, 20t, 23t, 26b, 27tb, 28b, 33t, 39t, 43t, 44t, 69t, 70t, 77b, 79, 83t, 99t, 108t, 110
Maurice Brown 19t
Christ Church School 8t, 9t, 37t, 70b, 74t
Darby and Joan Club 64t
Douglas Feast 84t
Graham Gower 63, 68b, 69b, 71b, 73b, 74b, 75tb, 76tb, 77t, 78tb, 80tb, 81tb, 82tb, 86t, 87b, 90b, 91tb
Brenda Hargreaves 87t, 97b, 100b, 101t
Keith Holdaway 83b, 84b, 85tb, 90t, 96t

Immanuel and St Andrew's School 86b, 93b, 94
Hilda Jones 38b
Audrey Mitchell 40b, 52b
Faye Norman vii
Cynthia Payne 88tb
Spires Centre 109b
Streatham Labour Party 95
Streatham Society/John Cresswell 106, 23b, 47, 49t, 62tb, 64b, 66b, 73t, 89tb, 92tb, 97t, 104t, 106b
Ujima Housing Association 100t
Wandsworth Local History Library 5tb, 43t, 46t

All other photographs are from the collection of Patrick Loobey. Our thanks are also extended to members of the Local History Group of the Streatham Society for their assistance with this project, and to Maurice Brown and Elizabeth Barrett, without whose help this book would not have been possible.